White Slave Children in Colonial America: Supplement to the Trilogy

Richard Hayes Phillips, Ph.D.

Copyright © 2021
by Richard Hayes Phillips
4 Fisher Street, Canton, New York 13617
All Rights Reserved

Paperback Edition Published by
Genealogical Publishing Company
Baltimore, Maryland
2021

ISBN 9780806321141

TABLE OF CONTENTS

AUTHOR'S PREFACE	vii
GUIDE TO THE INDEXES	ix
KIDS BROUGHT TO CHESAPEAKE BAY	
NOT THE KIDS	1
KIDS FROM LONDON	6
CLOSER MATCHES FROM LONDON	20
POSSIBLE MATCHES FROM LONDON	23
KIDS FROM ESSEX	26
KIDS FROM WILTSHIRE	33
KIDS FROM DORSET	37
KIDS FROM SOMERSET	41
KIDS FROM IRELAND	46
KIDS FROM ELSEWHERE	47
INDICTMENTS FOR KIDNAPPING	48
INDEX TO SHIP CAPTAINS	52
INDEX TO SHIP ARRIVALS	58
INDEX TO REVOLUTIONARIES	67
KIDS BROUGHT TO DELAWARE RIVER	
SHIPPING RECORDS	68
COURT RECORDS	69
BAPTISMAL RECORDS	78
MARRIAGE RECORDS	81
SURNAME INDEX	83

County Map of England and Wales, 1824, in its entirety. Children were taken from Ireland, Scotland, Cumberland, Lancashire, Cheshire, Gloucester, Somerset, Devon, Cornwall, Dorset, Wiltshire, Hampshire, Kent, Essex, Yorkshire, Durham, Northumberland, and Middlesex (the City of London).

AUTHOR'S PREFACE

When I was a very young man, my grandfather's favorite cousin correctly identified me as the only one of my generation who was deeply interested in our family history. Accordingly, when ancestors on my father's side passed away, many family records passed on to me.

One day there arrived in my mailbox an obituary for Joseph Harmon Phillips, my great-great-grandfather. He was born and raised in Randolph County, North Carolina. He learned the trade of carpentry as a teenager, and was "engaged in the business of building cotton mills." But having been born of poor white parents, "he had but little chance to get up or on in the world. Slavery was in front of him and the rich above him."

And so, in 1852, at the age of twenty, he and his younger brother, James A. Phillips, decided to migrate to a free state. They walked all the way to the Ohio River, crossed by boat to Cincinnati, and traveled by train to their sister's home in Hamilton County, Indiana. The entire clan migrated to Paola, Kansas in 1855, when first it was opened to white settlement. James and Joseph became renowned abolitionists, elected officials, and military officers during the Civil War. I knew there was more to the story.

It turned out that Joseph's father Stephen was an orphan – a classic brick wall in genealogy. His mother was Delilah Allred, whose ancestral line traced back to David Hambleton of Westburn, Lanarkshire, Scotland. David was captured by Cromwell's forces during the English Civil War, shipped to the New World in chains, and sold into slavery in 1652 at a sawmill on the coast of Maine. His youngest son, James Hambleton, from whom I am descended, was captured and sold into slavery in 1699 in Westmoreland County, Virginia:

> "James Hamelton, servant to James Bourn, is adjudged to be twelve years of age and is ordered to serve according to law."

It wasn't only James. More than 300 white children were brought before Westmoreland County Court to have their ages adjudged and be sentenced to servitude for a number of years according to age brackets established by law – the younger the child, the longer the sentence. These were children *without indentures* – without a written contract, *taken against their will.*

And this was only one county in Virginia. There were many other counties in both Maryland and Virginia where court records from this time period, c. 1660-1720, had survived. This was child trafficking, white slavery. The kids were identified by their names, and by their ages, in court records on a date certain. There needed to be an index devoted exclusively to them.

AUTHOR'S PREFACE

I called up Genealogical Publishing Company, and they put me through to Joe Garonzik. Within two days he agreed that if I would search all of those court records and expand my index, they would publish my work. As originally published, my index listed 5,290 kids in 26 counties of Maryland and Virginia.

One thing led to another. In the Library of Congress were long-forgotten photostats of handwritten copies of colonial shipping records thought to have been lost in a fire long ago. This told me the shires and counties in England, Scotland, Ireland and Massachusetts from which these children were transported. Knowing their real names, as best the court clerk could spell them, and their years of birth, as best the court judges could guess them, I could do a targeted search of the birth and baptismal records. If the name appeared only once, no more, no less, in the correct year, or very near to it, this was probably the kidnapped child.

Where most of the colonial records still existed, I could search for survivors, to see what became of the children who outlived their terms of servitude. I chose Charles County, Maryland, because: (1) nearly all the records had survived, and there were indexes to those that were lost; (2) there were many children without indentures, 872 in all, in the court records; (3) of these, 333 (38%) were owned by men who served, at one time or another, as judges on the Charles County Court; and (4) under Maryland law, penalties for recaptured runaways were harsh – ten additional days of servitude for each day's absence, plus additional time for the cost of "taking them up."

Thus arose what is informally known as the "White Slave Children Trilogy"

Without Indentures: Index to White Slave Children in Colonial Court Records

White Slave Children of Colonial Maryland and Virginia: Birth and Shipping Records

White Slave Children of Charles County, Maryland: The Search for Survivors

More records have come to my attention. All the parish registers for London, Essex, Gloucester, Wiltshire, Dorset and Somerset are now online, enabling me to complete my search for the birth places of the children. Dozens more captains of white slave ships have been identified from colonial records of Virginia. More than forty indictments for kidnapping have been found in the court records of London. More than 100 white children sold into servitude along the Delaware River have been found, some of whom have been matched with their baptismal or marriage records. All of these records are compiled in this supplement. So far as is known, this completes the data set for the trilogy.

GUIDE TO THE INDEXES

KIDS BROUGHT TO CHESAPEAKE BAY

NOT THE KIDS

These are baptismal records of children from Gloucestershire, England, matched up with their marriage or burial records, thus proving that that they are not the children with the same names who appeared without indentures in the courts of colonial Maryland and Virginia. When *"Birth and Shipping Records"* was published, I had not examined the marriage and death records for Gloucestershire. It was all I could do to search all the baptismal records. When the Mormons came to Bristol to collect vital records for their website, "they were denied access to the entire diocese" because of their doctrine of baptizing the dead. As a result, the baptismal records of eleven parish registers from the city of Bristol, all dating to the seventeenth century, all of them mostly legible, are missing entirely from the Mormon website, and another two are missing in part. Several country parishes are missing as well. To complete the data set, I took more than two thousand photographs of baptismal records at the Bristol Records Office and examined them after returning to America. I was thus unable, for Bristol or anywhere else in Gloucestershire, to cross-check the baptismal records with marriage records and death records, and so I warned my readers that "there may be cases of mistaken identity when matching these with the colonial court records of Maryland and Virginia." (ref. *"Birth and Shipping Records,"* pp. xviii-xix). Now these records are online at www.ancestry.com. I have cross-checked all 215 "Kids from Gloucester" in *"Birth and Shipping Records"* (pp. 83-110) and have proven that thirty-four of them are "Not the Kids." Fifteen of these have been located in the birth and baptismal records elsewhere in England.

KIDS FROM LONDON

These are birth and baptismal records of ninety-nine children from London, England, matched up with their court appearances in Maryland and Virginia at which they were sentenced to slavery. They are drawn entirely from a database entitled "London, England, Church of England Baptisms, Marriages and Burials, 1538-1812," compiled by London Metropolitan Archives, London, England. These are names that are missing from the Mormon website, and thus are not included in the original index to "Kids from London" that appeared in *"Birth and Shipping Records"* (pp. 138-190). In 1650 there were 400,000 people living in London, and in 1700 there were 575,000. It was beyond the capability of one historian to collect and examine all the baptismal records from this time period, and I warned my readers that I was obliged to settle for incomplete records (ref. *"Birth and Shipping Records,"* p. xix).

GUIDE TO THE INDEXES

CLOSER MATCHES FROM LONDON

These are birth and baptismal records of eighteen children from London, England, matched up with court appearances of children with the same name who were sentenced to slavery by the courts of Maryland and Virginia. The dates of birth or baptism are closer matches than those in the index to "Kids from Gloucester" that originally appeared in *"Birth and Shipping Records"* (pp. 83-110). No marriage or burial records were found for any of these children in Gloucestershire or London. Genealogists should search both names for evidence of ancestral lineage.

POSSIBLE MATCHES FROM LONDON

These are birth and baptismal records of twenty-two children from London, England, matched up with court appearances of children with the same name who were sentenced to slavery by the courts of Maryland and Virginia. The dates of birth or baptism are not more closely matched than those in the index to "Kids from Gloucester" that originally appeared in *"Birth and Shipping Records"* (pp. 83-110). No marriage or burial records were found for any of these children in Gloucestershire or London. Genealogists should search both names for evidence of ancestral lineage.

The indexes to kids from other locations that appear in *"Birth and Shipping Records"* were cross-checked for marriage and death records to begin with, and so there are far fewer cases of mistaken identity. However, genealogists should search the London database to see if the birth of a child with the same name turns up in the same time frame, just to be sure.

KIDS FROM ESSEX, ET SEQ.

There are indexes to forty-five children from Essex, twenty-nine from Wiltshire, twenty-three from Dorset, thirty-two from Somerset, one from Kent, one from Gloucester, and one from Cheshire, matched up with their court appearances in Maryland and Virginia at which they were sentenced to slavery. All of these have been cross-checked for marriage and death records. Also presented is an index to eight children from the parish of Lisburn, ten miles upstream from the heart of Belfast, matched up with their court appearances. This is the only surviving parish register dating to the seventeenth century in all of Northern Ireland. The search took four days, and the list was inadvertently omitted from *"Birth and Shipping Records."*

GUIDE TO THE INDEXES

INDICTMENTS FOR KIDNAPPING

Found on www.ancestry.com within a database entitled "Virginia Colonial Records, 1607-1853," these are typewritten abstracts of court records from Middlesex County, England. Bounded on the south by the River Thames and on the east by the River Lea, Middlesex contains the very heart of London. There are forty-one entries for kidnapping, primarily for the purpose of selling the victims into slavery in Virginia. I came upon these court records when searching this database for the name of Mathew Trim, commander of the *Judith*, the *Indy*, and the *Robert & Samuell*, identified by his kidnapping victims who were sentenced by the court in York County, Virginia.

SHIPPING RECORDS

These are revised versions of the "Index to Ship Captains" and the "Index to Ship Arrivals" that originally appeared in *"Without Indentures: Index to White Slave Children in Colonial Court Records"* (Genealogical Publishing Company, Baltimore, Maryland, 2013, pp. 250-256). The original information was drawn entirely from the court records of colonial Maryland and Virginia. The new information is drawn entirely from a database entitled "Virginia Colonial Records, 1607-1853," on www.ancestry.com. The additions and corrections are underlined. Also presented is a list of "Ship Arrivals in Philadelphia," drawn almost entirely from *"History of Chester County, Pennsylvania,"* by J. Smith Futhey and Gilbert Cope (Louis H. Everts, Philadelphia, 1881, p. 22). Ships and captains already known from the court records of Maryland and Virginia to be white slave ships and child traffickers are underlined.

INDEX TO REVOLUTIONARIES

These are additions to the "Index to Revolutionaries" that originally appeared in *"White Slave Children of Colonial Maryland and Virginia: Birth and Shipping Records"* (Genealogical Publishing Company, Baltimore, Maryland, 2015, pp. 267-299). There are seven new entries, including birth, marriage, and death records, the documented lineage back to a white slave child without indentures (whose name is capitalized), and the source providing proof of military service. If the soldier was a minuteman active on day one, 19 April 1775, this is duly noted.

GUIDE TO THE INDEXES

KIDS BROUGHT TO DELAWARE RIVER

SHIPPING RECORDS

This is a list of "Ship Arrivals in Philadelphia," drawn almost entirely from *"History of Chester County, Pennsylvania,"* by J. Smith Futhey and Gilbert Cope (Louis H. Everts, Philadelphia, 1881, p. 22). Ships and captains already known from the court records of Maryland and Virginia to be white slave ships and child traffickers are underlined.

COURT RECORDS

These are the court appearances at which kidnapped children were sentenced to servitude in Chester County, Pennsylvania and adjacent counties. There are more than one hundred children, a number which pales in comparison to Maryland and Virginia, but no doubt there were many more in the court records of Philadelphia, all of which, from this time period, have been lost. The court abstracts state the name of the child, the name of the owner, the date of the court appearance, the age of the child as adjudged by the court, the length of the term of servitude, and any conditions stipulated by the court.

BAPTISMAL RECORDS

These are records of initial court appearances at which kidnapped children were sentenced to servitude in Chester County, Pennsylvania and adjacent counties, matched up with their baptismal records identifying their parents and places of birth. They are distinctly the closest matches on the record. There are twenty-one of them, plus another three for whom we know the birth place but not the parents. Of these, fifteen are from Scotland, eight are from England, and one is from Ireland.

MARRIAGE RECORDS

Drawn from a variety of databases, these are marriage records of persons who, as children, had been ordered into servitude in Chester County, Pennsylvania. There are thirteen of them. In three cases, the marriages took place before their expected date of freedom as stipulated by the court, suggesting leniency on the part of their owners.

NOT THE KIDS

"England Births and Christenings, 1538-1975," International Genealogical Index, https://familysearch.org/search/collection/igi

"Gloucestershire, England, Church of England Baptisms, Marriages and Burials, 1538-1813," compiled by Gloucestershire Archives, Gloucester, England, https://www.ancestry.com/search/collections/gloucbmdearly/

Adams, Henry, son of Walter and Alice Adams, Baptized 19 January 1689, Pebworth, Gloucester, England
Addams, Henry, married Sarah Webb, 15 October 1717, Pebworth, Gloucester, England

Arnold, Joseph, son of John and Anne Arnold, Born 26 November 1670, Baptized 4 December 1670, Longhope, Gloucester, England
Arnold, Joseph, married Elizabeth Malson, 22 April 1700, Longhope, Gloucester, England

Baker, Richard, son of Richard Baker, Baptized 1 January 1661, Saint Nicholas, Gloucester, Gloucester, England
Baker, Richard, married Ann Attwood, 1 August 1694, Saint Nicholas, Gloucester, Gloucester, England

Clark, Edmund, son of Matthew Clark, Baptized 12 February 1687, Wotton under Edge, Gloucester, England
Clark, Edmund, married Ann Ismett, 15 August 1714, Wotton under Edge, Gloucester, England

Fowler, Catherine, daughter of Henery Fowler, Baptized 21 April 1686, Wotton under Edge, Gloucester, England
Fowler, Katherine, married Edward Shakespeare, 8 April 1711, Wotton under Edge, Gloucester, England

Gibbins, Thomas, son of Thomas Gibbins, Baptized 17 April 1670, Saint Mary de Crypt, Gloucester, England
Gibbins, Thomas, son of Thomas Gibbins, Baptized 22 June 1673, Saint Mary de Crypt, Gloucester, England
Gibbons, Thomas, married Joane Stephens, 17 September 1700, Gloucester, Saint Mary de Crypt, Gloucester, England

NOT THE KIDS

Greene, William, son of Willaim Greene, Baptized 13 June 1667,
 Newent, Gloucester, England
Greene, William, married Anne Newton, 12 February 1699/1700, Newent,
 Gloucester, England

Greenway, Elizabeth, daughter of Thomas and Rebeckah Greenway,
 Baptized 1654, Deerhurst, Gloucester, England
Greenway, Elizabeth, daughter of Thomas Greenway, buried
 11 November 1654, Deerhurst with Apperley, Gloucester, England

Hone, Elizabeth, daughter of Richard Hone, Baptized 9 March 1681,
 Brockworth, Gloucester, England
Hone, Elizabeth, married Thomas Hayes (?), 30 March 1702/03,
 Brockworth, Gloucester, England

Hughes, Catherine, daughter of Thomas Hughes, Baptized 30 August 1686,
 Hampnett, Gloucester, England
Hughes, Catherine, daughter of Thomas and Frediswid Hughes, buried
 30 August 1686, Hampnett, Gloucester, England
 [marriage record says "Frydeswid" – ed.]

Hughes, James, son of James and Sarah Hughes, Baptized 15 July 1689,
 Cirencester, Gloucester, England
Hughes, James "Junr.", buried 14 June 1724, Cirencester, Gloucester,
 England

Hughes, John, son of James Hughes, Baptized 13 April 1697,
 Cirencester, Gloucester, England
Hughes, John, son of James Hughes, buried 14 June 1700, Cirencester,
 Gloucester, England

Jeffris, Thomas, son of William and Mary Jeffris, Baptized
 30 November 1662, Cirencester, Gloucester, England
Jeffris, Thomas, married Mary Estington, 17 May 1687, Cirincester,
 Gloucester, England
Jeffris, Thomas, married Amy Austin, 20 December 1687, Cirincester,
 Gloucester, England

NOT THE KIDS

Jenkins, Thomas, son of Thomas and Sarah Jenkins, Baptized 5 February 1698/9, Dursley, Gloucester, England
Jenkins, Thomas, son of Thomas and Sarah Jenkins, buried 22 February 1698/9, Dursley, Gloucester, England

Jones, Edward, son of Thomas Jones, Baptized 3 August 1662, Wotton under Edge, Gloucester, England
Jones, Edward, married Elizabeth Crew, 4 April 1686, Wotton under Edge, Gloucester, England

Knight, Peterus, son of Johis and Annae Knight, Baptized 12 March 1692/3, Winchcombe, Gloucester, England
Knight, Peter, married Elizabeth Piggen, 3 October 1722, Winchcombe, Gloucester, England

Lane, Mary, parents not named, Baptized 31 March 1667, Chipping Campden, Gloucester, England
Lane, Mary, married Richard Fifield, 22 July 1695, Chipping Camden, Gloucester, England

Mason, Richard, son of George Mason, Baptized 22 December 1667, Bisley, Gloucester, England
Mason, Richard, married Mary Coats, 23 April 1699, Bisley, Gloucester, England

Miles, Nathaniell, son of Joseph Miles, Baptized 2 August 1663, Eastington and Alkerton, Gloucester, England
Miles, Nathaniell, married Ann Gabb, 1 October 1697, Eastington, Gloucester, England

Morgan, Katharine, daughter of Henry and Anne Morgan, Baptized 7 June 1682, Maiseyhampton, Gloucester, England
Morgan, Catherine, married Clement Furly, 13 June 1710, Maiseyhampton, Gloucester, England

Neale, Arthur, son of Arthur Neale, Baptized 22 February 1684, Thornbury, Gloucester, England
Neal, Arthur, married Hester Holly, 2 May 1709, Thornbury, Gloucester, England

NOT THE KIDS

Neale, Robert, son of William Neale, Baptized 14 October 1666, Hawkesbury, Gloucester, England
Neale, Robert, married Mary Parly, 14 April 1691, Hawkesbury, Gloucester, England

Painter, John, son of William Painter, Baptized 6 November 1682, Oxenhall, Gloucester, England
Painter, John, son of William Painter "of Oxenhall," buried 20 April 1683, Newent, Gloucester, England

Perkins, William, son of William and Lydia Perkins, Baptized 21 February 1685, Cam, Gloucester, England
Perkins, William, married Abigall Bendall, 13 May 1718, Cam, Gloucester, England

Price, John, son of William and Anne Price, Baptized 6 August 1693, Awre with Blakeney, Gloucester, England
Priece, John, married Elizabeth Phelps, 27 September 1720, Awre, Gloucester, England

Read, Elizabeth, parents not named, Baptized 4 March 1676, Ebrington, Gloucester, England
Read, Elizabeth, buried 13 October 1703, Ebrington, Gloucester, England

Redinge, John, son of Richard Redinge, Baptized 11 March 1668, Dymock, Gloucester, England
Redinge, John, son of John Redinge, Baptized 25 January 1692, Dymock, Gloucester, England

Shaile, Thomas, son of Thomas Shaile, Born 23 March 1675, Awre with Blakeney, Gloucester, England
Shail, Thomas, married Jane Fisher, 26 November 1702, Awre, Gloucester, England

Smyth, Daniel, son of Peter Smyth, Baptized 8 June 1673, North Nibley, Gloucester, England
Smyth, Daniel, married Mary Riddiford, 12 May 1695, North Nibley, Gloucester, England

NOT THE KIDS

Sturey (?), John, son of John Sturey (?), Baptized 5 May 1683, Iron Acton, Gloucester, England
[Cannot verify the baptismal record – ed.]

Tracie, John, son of Melchizedek Tracie, Baptized 15 January 1688/9, Chipping Campden, Gloucester, England
Tracey, John, married Sarah Huntt, 30 October 1715, Chipping Campden, Gloucester, England

Upton, Thomas, son of Thomas and Rose Upton, Baptized 7 December 1690, Sherrington, Gloucester, England
Upton, Thomas, son of Thomas Upton, buried 22 July 1705, Sherrington, Gloucester, England

White, Thomas, son of John White, Baptized 15 July 1650, Dymock, Gloucester, England OK
White, Thomas, son of John White, buried 15 December 1682, Dymock, Gloucester, England

Woolles, William, son of William Woolles, Baptized 17 August 1663, Mitcheldean, Gloucester, England
Wooles, William, married Sara Spenser, 11 May 1691, Mitcheldean, Gloucester, England

---

Fifteen of these thirty-four children have been located elsewhere, each of their birth or baptismal records being distinctly the closest match on the record, with no marriage or death record existing:

Cheshire: Thomas Upton

Dorset: Peter Knight

Essex: Richard Mason

Gloucester: Arthur Neale

London: Henry Adams, Joseph Arnold, Richard Baker, Catherine Fowler, Katharine Morgan, William Perkins, John Reading, Daniell Smyth, Thomas White

Wiltshire: Elizabeth Greeneway, Thomas Jeffreyes

KIDS FROM LONDON

"London, England, Church of England Baptisms, Marriages and Burials, 1538-1812," compiled by London Metropolitan Archives, London, England, https://www.ancestry.com/search/collections/lmaearlyparish/

"Without Indentures: Index to White Slave Children in Colonial Court Records," Richard Hayes Phillips, Ph.D., Genealogical Publishing Co., 2013.

Adams, Henry, son of Frances and Mary Adams, Baptized 2 March 1687/8, Saint Katherine Cree, City of London
Adams, Henry, 5 July 1699, age 11, Princess Anne County, Virginia, William Shipp

Adcocks, Elizabeth, daughter of Edward and Merrell Adcocks, Baptized 17 December 1671, Saint Sepulchre, Holborn, City of London
Adcock, Elizabeth, 5 May 1685, age 12, Surry County, Virginia, Thomas Blunt, "who came into this Country in the Brothers Adventure, Henry Trigany, Master, the beginning of November last"

Eyler, Mary, daughter of Francis Eyler, Baptized 4 February 1665/6, All Hallows Staining, City of London
Ailer, Mary, 9 March 1680, age 14, Charles County, Maryland, Francis Wyne

Anderson, Roger, son of Roger and Elizabeth Anderson, Baptized 18 February 1713, Saint Mary the Virgin, Twickenham, Richmond upon Thames, Kent
Anderson, Roger, 15 June 1725, age 12, Somerset County, Maryland, Capt. James Lindow, "Imported into this Country in the Sloop Called John of Doublin"

Arnold, Joseph, son of John and Margaret, Born 7 January 1672/3, Baptized 19 January 1672/3, Saint Giles, Cripplegate, City of London
Arnold, Joseph, 10 August 1687, (age 15), Lancaster County, Virginia, William Therriatt, nine years

KIDS FROM LONDON

Austin, Edward, son of Edward and Joane Austin, Baptized 8 May 1660,
	Saint Magnus the Martyr, City of London [1]
Austin, Edward, 28 February 1677, age 16, Talbot County, Maryland,
	Richard Carlton, seven years

Baker, Richard, son of Richard Baker, Baptized 7 October 1660,
	Saint Olave, Bermondsey, Southwark, Surrey
Baker, Richard, 4 February 1678, age 17, Middlesex County, Virginia,
	John Vaus, "comeing into this Countrey in ye Ship, Duke of Yorke"

Ballstar, John, son of John and Winnifruite (sic) Ballstar, Baptized
	5 March 1703/4, Saint Mary, Whitechapel, Tower Hamlets,
	Middlesex
Ballister, John, 10 March 1719, age 15, Anne Arundel County,
	Richard Franklin

Barrock, John, son of Phillip and Elizabeth Barrock, Born
	2 September 1660, Baptized 9 September 1660, Saint John
	of Wapping, Tower Hamlets, Middlesex
Barrick, John, 17 January 1665, age under 15, Talbot County, Maryland,
	Henery Coursey, seven years, "to bee free" 29 November 1672

Barton, George, son of John Barton, Baptized 15 November 1649,
	Saint Giles, Camberwell, Southwark, Surrey
Barton, George, 10 March 1674, age 21-22, Charles County, Maryland,
	Zachary Wade

Berks, John, son of Nathanael and Jane Berks, Baptized 16 August 1685,
	Saint Olave, Bermondsey, Southwark, Surrey
Birk, John, 16 November 1698, age 13, Northumberland County, Virginia,
	James Waddy

Bridgeman, Thomas, son of John and Jane Bridgeman, Baptized
	18 April 1652, Saint Benet Gracechurch, City of London
Bridgeman, Thomas, 20 June 1663, age 13, Northumberland County,
	Virginia, Capt. William Nutt

---

[1] See also Kids from Portsmouth, in *"Birth and Shipping Records"*

KIDS FROM LONDON

Brookes, Kathrine, daughter of John Brookes, Baptized 6 October 1678,
Saint Alfege, Greenwich, London
Brookes, Katherine, 3 July 1689, age 13, Old Rappahannock County,'
Virginia, Henry Lucas

Burck, William, son of John Burck, Baptized 30 August 1696,
Saint Mary Magdalen, Bermondsey, Southwark, Surrey
Burck, William, 31 May 1710, age 13, Westmoreland County, Virginia,
Robert Lovell

Birkes, Edward, son of John and Mary Birkes, Baptized 25 May 1707,
Saint Giles, Cripplegate, City of London
Burk, Edward, 24 March 1719, **age 10, Queen Anne's County, Maryland,**
John Cobreath

Burck, John, son of John Burck, Baptized 12 March 1658,
Saint Mary the Virgin, Harefield, Hillingdon, Middlesex
Burke, John, 9 March 1675, age 15, Charles County, Maryland,
Anne Fowke, by James Hoorn (?)

Birks, John, son of John and Mary Birks, Baptized 25 February 1700/1,
All Hallows the Great, City of London
Burke, John, 8 June 1708, age 9, Somerset County, Maryland,
Alexander Madux

Cammell, Samuel, son of Timothy and Amey Cammell, Baptized
17 April 1684, Saint Giles, Cripplegate, City of London
Cammell, Samuell, 22 June 1699, age 18, Northumberland County, Virginia,
Christopher Garlington

Cane, John, son of John and Elizabeth Cane, Baptized 5 December 1644,
"9 Dayes old," Saint Dunstan and All Saints, Stepney,
Tower Hamlets, Middlesex
Canes, John, 11 March 1663, (age 18), Lancaster County, Virginia,
Bryan Stott, six years

Covey, James, son of Charles and Cinley (sic) Covey, Baptized
21 November 1671, Saint Giles, Cripplegate, City of London
Coffey, James, 19 February 1683, age 11, Accomack County, Virginia,
William Nock

8

KIDS FROM LONDON

Cole, Ambrose, son of James and Susanah Cole, Born and Baptized
 21 September 1657, Saint Andrew, Holborn, Camden, London
Collie, Ambrose, 6 July 1674, age 16, Middlesex County, Virginia,
 Thomas Townsend

Crane, Jane, daughter of Thomas and Margarett Crane, Baptized
 30 August 1672, Saint John the Baptist, Hillingdon, Middlesex
Crane, Jane, 22 May 1689, age 15, Northumberland County, Virginia,
 Richard Rogers, declaring that he bought her "to serve him
 six years and no longer"

Dowell, Richard, son of Joshua and Elizabeth Dowell, Born and Baptized
 24 May 1664, Saint John of Wapping, Tower Hamlets, Middlesex
Dowell, Richard, 24 June 1680, age 17, York County, Virginia,
 Joseph Bing, "he coming in the Rose & Crown,
 Capt. Barth Clements, Commander"

Draper, Ralph, son of John (?) Draper, Baptized 19 February 1666/7,
 Saint John at Hampstead, Camden, Middlesex
Draper, Raiph, 14 June 1681, age 16, Charles County, Maryland,
 Philip Lines

Tuffe, Charles, son of Ralph Tuffe, Baptized 10 September 1677,
 Saint George the Martyr, Southwark, Surrey
Duffee, Charles, 19 June 1694, Accomack County, Virginia,
 age 15, John Parker, Jr.

Dyal, John, son of Simon and Sarah Dyal, Baptized 17 October 1704,
 Saint Mary, Whitechapel, Tower Hamlets, Middlesex
Dyal, John, 12 June 1722, age 15, Charles County, Maryland, George Elgin

Evelling, Henry, son of Abraham and Jane Evelling, Baptized
 8 October 1643, Saint Giles in the Fields, Holborn, Camden
Evlyn, Henry, 11 May 1663, (age 17), Lancaster County, Virginia,
 Ever Peterson, seven years

Fewell, Stephen, son of William Fewell, Born and Baptized
 7 November 1653, Saint Olave, Bermondsay, Southwark, Surrey
Fewell, Stephen, 24 April 1671, age 17, York County, Virginia,
 Edmund Chisman, Jr., "imported in the Rebecca,
 by Capt. Christopher Evoling, Commander"

KIDS FROM LONDON

Foote, James, son of John and Anne Foote, Born and Baptized
2 August 1651, Saint Mary, Stratford Bow, Tower Hamlets, Middlesex
Foote, James, 25 January 1669, age 17, York County, Virginia,
Thomas Dennett (seven years)

Fowler, Kathrin, daughter of Thymothy and Mary Fowler, Baptized
4 November 1688, Saint James, Clerkenwell, Islington, Middlesex
Fowler, Catherine, 20 June 1699, age 13, Talbot County, Maryland,
John Allexander

Freeman, Henry, son of Henry and Mary Freeman, Baptized
20 January 1666/7, Saint Olave, Bermondsey, Southwark, Surrey
Freeman, Henry, 26 January 1680, age 14, York County, Virginia,
John Parsons, "comeing this yeare in the Dimond"

Gaton, Thomas, son of Walter and Sarah Gaton, Baptized 25 April 1669,
Saint Giles in the Fields, Holborn, Camden [2]
Gaton, Thomas, 7 September 1680, age 12, Surry County, Virginia,
Coll. Thomas Swann, "who came in the last Shipping"

Gosh, Richard, son of Thomas Gosh, Baptized 15 October 1664,
Saint Mary, Newington, Southwark, Surrey
Gosh, Richard, 8 January 1678, age 15, Charles County, Maryland,
Peter Car, by Joseph Bullott

Gregorie, Nicholas, son of Nicholas Gregorie, Baptized 14 May 1665,
Saint Mary, Battersea, Wandsworth, Surrey
Gregory, Nicholas, 24 February 1679, age 13, York County, Virginia,
Joseph Bing, "imported in the Golden Fortune,
Capt. William Jeffreys, Commander," eleven years

Grove, George, son of William and Mary Grove, Baptized 16 May 1675,
Saint Saviour, Southwark, Surrey
Groves, George, 12 January 1686, age 11, Charles County, Maryland,
Edward Evans

---

[2] See also Kids from Humberside, in *"Birth and Shipping Records"*

KIDS FROM LONDON

Harbe, John, son of John and Rebekah Harbe, Baptized 15 September 1671,
    Saint Martin Outwich, City of London
Harbey, John, 24 October 1683, age 12, York County, Virginia,
    John Martin, "imported in the Humphrey & Elizabeth,"
    Capt. John Martin, Commander

Herry, George, son of Gabrille and Dorrithe Herry, Baptized 20 July 1655,
    Saint Bartholomew the Great, City of London
Harry, George, 24 August 1669, age 17, Northumberland County, Virginia,
    Sym. Richardson

Hatton, George, son of William and Mary Hatton, Baptized
    24 September 1665, Saint Giles in the Fields, Holborn, Camden
Hatton, George, 3 June 1678, age 12, Charles City County, Virginia,
    James Thwait

Hughes, Nicholas, son of Nicholas Hughes, Baptized 15 September 1657,
    Saint Mary, Bromley Saint Leonard, Tower Hamlets, Middlesex
Hewes, Nicholas, 16 June 1675, age 16, Northumberland County, Virginia,
    Collo. St. Leger Codd

Hughes, George, son of Thomas and Margaret Hughes, Baptized
    30 October 1664, Saint Dunstan in the West, City of London
Hewis, George, 8 December 1679, age 18, Middlesex County, Virginia,
    William Dudley, "comeing into this Country in ye Shipp,
    Owners Advice" [Owners Adventure – ed.]

Hankes, Dorothy, daughter of Edward and Dorothy Hankes, Baptized
    26 January 1650/1, Saint Giles in the Fields, Holborn, Camden
Hincks, Dorothy, 12 January 1669, age 19, Charles County, Maryland,
    John Wheeler

Hopkins, Henry, son of Henry Hopkins, Baptized 30 January 1678/9,
    Saint Nicholas, Deptford, Greenwich, Kent
Hopkins, Henry, 21 June 1693, age 14, Northumberland County, Virginia,
    Thomas Baker

KIDS FROM LONDON

Hewson, Richard, son of William and Katherin Hewson, Baptized
    22 June 1651, Saint Mary Woolnoth, City of London [3]
Huson, Richard, 15 March 1670, (age 15-18), Talbot County, Maryland,
    Joseph Wickes, six years

Jenkins, David, son of William and Margrit Jenkins, Baptized
    4 October 1655, Saint Ann Blackfriars, City of London
Jenkins, David, 24 July 1674, age 17, York County, Virginia,
    William Townsend, imported in the Industry, "by Capt.
    Phineas Hide," Commander, seven years

Jobson, Thomas, son of John Jobson, Baptized 12 January 1673,
    Saint Mary Magdalen, Bermondsey, Southwark, Surrey [4]
Jobson, Thomas, (torn) June 1683, age 12, Talbot County, Maryland,
    John Newman

Johnson, George, son of Herbert and Ann Johnson, Baptized
    25 April 1659, Saint Dunstan in the West, City of London
Johnson, George, 12 May 1674, (age 16), Lancaster County, Virginia,
    Lt. Coll. John Carter, eight years

Jordan, Henry, son of Henry and Mary Jordan, Baptized 28 February 1668/9,
    Saint Giles in the Fields, Holborn, Camden
Jordan, Henry, 24 November 1685, age 16, Kent County, Maryland,
    Robert Perk

Kilbee, John, son of Richard and Barbarie Kilbee, Baptized
    6 January 1657/8, St. Michael, Highgate, Camden, Middlesex
Keelby, John, 10 June 1674, age 16, Charles County, Maryland,
    Peter Carr

---

[3] See also Kids from Lancashire, in *"Birth and Shipping Records"*

[4] See also Kids from Durham, in *"Birth and Shipping Records"*

KIDS FROM LONDON

Keene, Thomas, son of Thomas Keene, Born 2 January 1660/1, Baptized
    6 January 1660/1, Saint Olave, Bermondsey, Southwark, Surrey [5]
Keene, Thomas, 17 June 1673, (age 14), Talbot County, Maryland,
    William Gary, eight years

Kemp, William, son of Richard and Isabell Kemp, Baptized
    26 January 1656/7, Saint Botolph, Bishopsgate, City of London
Kemp, William, 17 April 1672, age 17, Accomack County, Virginia,
    Roger Mackeel

Kenny, John, son of Dennis Kenny, Baptized 13 March 1691/2,
    Saint Mary at Lambeth, Lambeth, Surry
Kenney, John, 20 August 1700, age 11, Talbot County, Maryland,
    Michaell Earle

Lawrence, Will, son of Thomas and Rebeca Lawrence, Baptized
    10 May 1652, Saint Margaret, Uxbridge, Hillingdon, Middlesex
Laurance, William, 17 June 1673, (age 18-22), Talbot County, Maryland,
    William Steevens, six years

Male, Catherine, daughter of Robert and Catherine Male,
    Born 16 May 1663, Baptized 29 May 1663, Saint Gregory
    by Saint Paul, City of London
Maley, Katherin, 20 January 1680, age 16, Talbot County, Maryland,
    Thomas Anderson

Mare, Charles, son of Thomas and Jane Mare, Baptized 6 March 1665/6,
    Saint Olave, Hart Street, City of London
Mar, Charles, 24 March 1679, age 14, York County, Virginia,
    Anthony Seabrell, "came in the Constant" [Constant Mary – ed.]

Mere, John, son of John and Anne Mere, Baptized 23 July 1695,
    Saint Dunstan and All Saints, Stepney, Tower Hamlets, Middlesex
Meer, John, 17 June 1707, age 12, Talbot County, Maryland, Joseph Gough

---

[5] See also Kids from Cornwall, in *"Birth and Shipping Records"*

KIDS FROM LONDON

Mountford, William, son of William and Francis Mountford, Baptized
16 August 1668, Collegiate Church of Saint Katherine
by the Tower, City of London
Montfort, William, 14 June 1682, age 16, Westmoreland County, Virginia,
Thomas Kirton

Morgan, Katharine, daughter of Thomas Morgan, Baptized 10 October 1680,
Collegiate Church of Saint Katherine by the Tower, City of London
Morgan, Catherine, 14 June 1699, age 18, Lancaster County, Virginia,
Thomas Martin, six years

Mortton, Georg, son of Georg and Ann Mortton, Born 1 August 1660,
Baptized 12 August 1660, Saint Leonard, Shoreditch, Hackney,
Middlesex
Morton, George, 10 November 1670, age 11, York County, Virginia,
William Bell, "imported in the Tryall of Bristol"

Mosle, William, son of William Mosle, Baptized 12 January 1664/5,
Saint Mary Magdalen, Bermondsey, Southwark, Surrey
Mosely, William, 27 February 1679, age 13, Northampton County, Virginia,
John Bellamy

Mugg, Thomas, son of Thomas and Margaret Mugg, Born
25 February 1659/60, Baptized 13 March 1659/60,
Saint Mary, Stratford Bow, Tower Hamlets, Middlesex
Mugg, Thomas, 8 December 1679, age 17, Middlesex County, Virginia,
Coll. Mathew Kempe, "comeing into this Country in ye Shipp,
Owners Advice" [Owners Adventure – ed.]

Newell, James, son of John Newell, Baptized 13 October 1650,
Saint Olave, Bermondsey, Southwark, Surrey
Newall, James, 12 July 1664, age 14, Charles County, Maryland,
George Bradshaw

Nicholes, Richard, son of John and Ann Nicholes, Baptized
18 September 1664, Saint Olave, Bermondsey, Southwark, Surrey
Nicholes, Richard, 16 February 1677, age 14, Accomack County, Virginia,
William Nock

KIDS FROM LONDON

Ould, John, son of William and Susann Ould, Baptized 13 April 1669,
    Saint Saviour, Southwark, Surrey
Old, John, 6 February 1683, age 13, Old Rappahannock County,
    Edward Chilton

Osburne, Henry, son of Thomas and Joane Osburne, Baptized
    23 January 1670/1, Saint Saviour, Southwark, Surrey
Osburne, Henry, 4 March 1685, age 15, Old Rappahannock County,
    Virginia, Ralph Nell

Osborn, Mathew, son of William Osborn, Baptized 29 September 1661,
    Saint Peter and Saint Paul, Harlington, Hillington, Middlesex
Osburne, Mathew, 7 February 1673, age 11, Accomack County, Virginia,
    Capt. Daniell Jenifer

Págg, Márgery, daughter of Edwárd and Katherine Págg, Baptized
    21 June 1646, Saint Leonard, Shoreditch, Hackney, Middlesex
Page, Margerie, 5 January 1664, age 19, Charles County, Maryland,
    Walter Beane

Paine, Edward, son of Edward Paine, Baptized 23 August 1670,
    Saint Nicholas, Deptford, Greenwich, Kent
Paine, Edward, 26 November 1684, age 13, Westmoreland County,
    Virginia, Joseph Beale

Paine, Richard, son of John and Margrett Paine, Baptized 14 May 1654,
    Saint Giles in the Fields, Holborn, Camden
Paine, Richard, 15 February 1667, age 13, Norfolk County, Virginia,
    William Carter

Pen, John, son of John and Gartrude Pen, Baptized 14 July 1642,
    Saint Dunstan and All Saints, Stepney, Tower Hamlets, Middlesex
Penn, John, 12 March 1662, (age 17), Lancaster County, Virginia,
    Widow of Daniel Johnson, deceased, seven years

Perkins, William, son of Humphrey and Bridget Perkins, Baptized
    24 February 1685/6, Saint Andrew, Holborn, Camden, London
Perkins, William, 11 August 1702, age 16, Charles County, Maryland,
    Samuell Luckett

KIDS FROM LONDON

Poor, Robert, son of Robert and Catherine Poor, Baptized 26 July 1685,
    Saint Mary, Hampton, Richmond upon Thames, Middlesex
Poor, Robert, 26 April 1699, age 15, Westmoreland County, Virginia,
    Robert Redman

Prat, Thomas, son of Thomas and Ann Prat, Baptized 19 June 1664,
    Saint John at Hackney, Hackney, Middlesex
Pratt, Thomas, 24 March 1679, age 15, York County, Virginia,
    Anthony Seabrell, "came in the Constant" [Constant Mary – ed.]

Reading, John, son of Roger and Ann Reading, Baptized 27 December 1668,
    Saint Giles in the Fields, Holborn, Camden
Reading, John, 2 April 1678, age 9, Kent County, Maryland,
    Robertt Perke

Russell, Katherin, daughter of Henry and Anne Russell, Baptized
    3 December 1664, Saint Dunstan and All Saints, Stepney,
    Tower Hamlets, Middlesex
Russell, Kathren, 30 April 1678, age 15, Talbot County, Maryland,
    Thomas Badell, seven years

Rye, John, son of John and Carolina Rye, Baptized 21 February 1687/8,
    Saint Alfege, Greenwich, London
Rye, John, 8 August 1699, age 12, Charles County, Maryland,
    Capt. John Bayne

Salisbury, Elizabeth, daughter of Nathaniell and Grace Salisbury, Baptized
    12 June 1664, Saint Giles in the Fields, Holborn, Camden
Salisbury, Elizabeth, 6 January 1674, age 10, Accomack County, Virginia,
    Robert Hewett

Sanders, Edward, son of Edward Sanders, Baptized 24 November 1655,
    Saint Olave, Bermondsey, Southwark, Surrey
Sander, Edward, 10 March 1669, age 16, York County, Virginia,
    John Whysken, eight years

Simmons, William, son of Ephraim Simmons, Baptized 12 January 1689/90,
    Saint Nicholas, Deptford, Greenwich, Kent
Simmons, William, 13 February 1700, age 12, Charles County, Maryland,
    Samuel Luckett

KIDS FROM LONDON

Simpson, Jane, daughter of Nicholas and Mary Simpson, Baptized
    28 August 1653, Saint Dunstan and All Saints, Stepney,
    Tower Hamlets, Middlesex
Simpson, Jane, 9 September 1668, (age 15), Lancaster County, Virginia,
    John Simpson, nine years

Smyth, Daniell, son of William and Katherine Smyth, Baptized
    27 November 1671, All Hallows the Great, City of London
Smith, Daniell, 15 June 1686, age 14, Talbot County, Maryland,
    John Stanley

Stanley, Jonathan, son of Peter and Elizabeth Stanley, Baptized
    22 November 1649, Saint Giles in the Fields, Holborn, Camden
Stanley, Jonathan, 8 July 1668, age 15, Lancaster County, Virginia,
    Humphrey Jones, nine years

Steedman, Edward, son of Edmund Steedman, Baptized 7 April 1664,
    Saint Mary at Lambeth, Lambeth, Surrey, England
Stidman, Edward, 12 June 1677, age 14, Charles County, Maryland,
    Capt. Ignatius Causin

Styles, William, son of George and Jesesa (sic) Styles, Baptized
    24 August 1662, Saint Mary, Staines, Surrey
Styles, William, 4 March 1679, age 17, Northampton County, Virginia,
    Hancock Lee

Taylor, Samuel, son of Samuel and Elizabeth Taylor, Baptized
    29 October 1663, Saint Gregory by Saint Paul, City of London
Taylor, Samuell, 18 March 1679, age 14, Talbot County, Maryland,
    William Wintersell, eight years

Thomas, Rowland, son of John Thomas, Baptized 29 January 1659/60,
    Saint Dunstan in the West, City of London
Thomas, Rowland, 6 July 1674, age 13, Middlesex County, Virginia,
    Major John Burnham

KIDS FROM LONDON

Vaughan, John, son of Thomas and Mary Vaughan, Baptized 7 June 1659,
   Saint Dunstan in the West, City of London
Vaughan, John, 25 January 1675, age 16, York County, Virginia,
   Anne Dennett, "imported in the George, Capt. Thomas Grantham,
   Commander," eight years

Watts, Thomas, son of Richard Watts, Baptized 30 November 1651,
   Saint Olave, Bermondsey, Southwark, Surrey
Watts, Thomas, 15 February 1667, age 16, Norfolk County, Virginia,
   William Goldsmith

Watson, Richard, son of Thomas Watson, Baptized 22 August 1669,
   Saint Thomas, Southwark, Surrey
Wattson, Richard, (torn) 1685, age 15, Talbot County, Maryland,
   John Dickinson

Web, Samuell, son of Samuell and Jane Web, Baptized 11 February 1648/9,
   Saint Botolph, Bishopsgate, City of London
Webb, Samuell, 3 May 1660, age 13, Northumberland County, Virginia,
   Major George Colclough, eight years

Wiffin, John, son of Richard Wiffin, Baptized 6 November 1659,
   Saint Olave, Bermondsey, Southwark, Surrey
Whiffin, John, 8 July 1674, (age 16), Lancaster County, Virginia,
   Lt. Coll. John Carter, eight years

Wheldon, John, son of Thomas and Jane Wheldon, Baptized
   27 November 1642, Saint Giles in the Fields, Holborn, Camden
Whilden, John, 11 June 1667, age 24, Charles County, Maryland,
   Edward Swanne

White, Thomas, son of Samuell and Judith White, Baptized 19 June 1649,
   Saint Mary Woolnoth, City of London
White, Thomas, 8 January 1668, (age 18), Lancaster County, Virginia,
   Richard Parrett, six years

Wild, Thomas, son of Thomas Wild, Born 30 October 1655,
   Saint Mary, Harrow, Harrow, Middlesex
Wild, Thomas, 15 June 1675, (age 18-22), Talbot County, Maryland,
   Robert Noble and Simon Steephen, six years

KIDS FROM LONDON

Williams, Leonard, son of John and Jane Williams, Baptized
25 July 1669, Saint Dunstan in the West, City of London
Williams, Leonard, 17 May 1681, age 11, Accomack County, Virginia,
William Anderson

Willmott, Bartholomew, son of Jerman (?) and Katherine Willmott,
Baptized 5 June 1645, Saint Dunstan in the West, City of London
Willmott, Bartholomew, 13 November 1667, age 19, Lancaster County,
Virginia, Coll. John Carter, Esqr., two (sic) years

Wilson, Cristhop (sic), son of Daniel and Ann Wilson, Baptized 3 June 1683,
Saint Dunstan in the West, City of London
Wilson, Christopher, 4 April 1694, age 11, Northumberland County,
Virginia, Abraham Sheers

Wood, Mychaell, son of Mychaell Wood, Baptized 23 May 1684,
"10 months old" [born July 1683 – ed.],
Saint Mary Magdalen, Bermondsey, Southwark, Surrey
Wood, Michaell, 19 January 1699, age 15, Northumberland County,
Virginia, Capt. William Jones

Woodman, Joseph, son of Joseph Woodman, Baptized 13 April 1645,
Saint Andrew by the Wardrobe, City of London
Woodman, Joseph, 26 February 1661, age 14, Northumberland County,
Virginia, Henry Corbyn, seven years

Woodman, John, son of Mathew and Francis Woodman, Baptized
19 October 1671, Saint Mary, Hayes, Hillingdon, Middlesex
Woodman, John, 4 November 1685, age 14, Old Rappahannock County,
Francis Sterne

CLOSER MATCHES FROM LONDON

"London, England, Church of England Baptisms, Marriages and Burials, 1538-1812," compiled by London Metropolitan Archives, London, England, https://www.ancestry.com/search/collections/lmaearlyparish/

"England Births and Christenings, 1538-1975," International Genealogical Index, https://familysearch.org/search/collection/igi

"Without Indentures: Index to White Slave Children in Colonial Court Records," Richard Hayes Phillips, Ph.D., Genealogical Publishing Co., 2013.

Adams, William, son of Edward and Susana Adams, Baptized 5 May 1658, Saint Dunstan and All Saints, Stepney, Tower Hamlets, Middlesex
Adams, William, 6 February 1673, age 14, Accomack County, Virginia, Peter Walker

Atkins, John, son of John and Mary, Baptized 12 April 1661, Saint Botolph Aldersgate, City of London
Atkins, John, 20 July 1670, age 9, Northumberland County, Virginia, Thomas Williams

Chambers, Richard, son of Thomas and Katherine, Baptized 30 January 1684/5, Saint Saviour, Southwark, Surrey
Chambers, Richard, 15 March 1698, age 12, Talbot County, Maryland, Volentine Carter

Davies, John, son of Joel Davies, Baptized August 1, 1686, Saint Mary at Lambeth, Lambeth, Surrey
Davies, John, 25 January 1699, age 12, Westmoreland County, Virginia, Peter Smith

Davis, Edward, son of John and Mary Davis, Baptized 1 March 1701/2, Saint Botolph, Bishopsgate, City of London
Davis, Edward, 5 June 1716, age 14, Talbot County, Maryland, Peter Webb, "he alleges he has" Indentures "but cannot now produce them"

Dobbins, Richard, son of Richard Dobbins, Baptized 13 November 1682, Saint Mary the Virgin, Harefield, Hillingdon, Middlesex
Dobin, Richard, 31 May 1699, age 16, Westmoreland County, Virginia, Thomas Brown

CLOSER MATCHES FROM LONDON

Ellis, Henery, son of Robert Ellis, Baptized 1 August 1648,
    Saint Alfege, Greenwich, City of London
Ellis, Henry, 24 January 1660, age 11, York County, Virginia,
    Thomas Heynes, ten years

English, John, son of John and Easter English, Born and Baptized
    13 May 1657, Saint Pancras, Soper Lane, City of London
English, John, 13 June 1671, age 14, Somerset County, Maryland,
    Christopher Nutter

Gilson, William, son of Thomas Gilson, Baptized 16 May 1649,
    Saint Saviour, Southwark, Surrey
Gilson, William, 10 June 1668, age 18, Lancaster County, Virginia,
    William Hutchins, six years

Hicks, John, son of Robert and Elizabeth Hicks, Baptized 5 October 1661,
    Saint Dunstan in the East, City of London
Hicks, John, 19 March 1679, age 17, Northumberland County, Virginia,
    Robert Sech

Mason, Thomas, son of Richard and Damaris Mason, Baptized
    9 August 1657, Saint Botolph, Aldgate, City of London
Mason, Thomas, 15 February 1669, age 12, Norfolk County, Virginia,
    William Handcock

Newman, Charles, son of Henery and Dorothie Newman, Baptized
    21 August 1664, Saint John at Hackney, Hackney, Middlesex
Newman, Charles, 27 March 1677, age 13 "& a halfe," Kent County,
    Maryland, Francis Finch

Palmer, John, son of John and Jane Palmer, Baptized 24 November 1644,
    Saint Giles in the Fields, Holborn, Camden
Palmer, John, 31 October 1661, age 16, York County, Virginia,
    Mrs. Mary Ludlow, five years

Parsons, Richard, son of John and Elizabeth Parsons, Baptized
    21 July 1652, Saint Botolph, Aldgate, City of London
Parson, Richard, 1 April 1669, age 16, Norfolk County, Virginia,
    George Minchon

CLOSER MATCHES FROM LONDON

Peirce, James, son of James and Mary Peirce, Baptized 2 January 1684,
 All Hallows, Barking by the Tower, City of London
Peirce, James, 13 July 1698, age 14, Lancaster County, Virginia,
 Andrew Jackson, ten years

Price, John, son of John and Elizabeth Price, Baptized 19 September 1666,
 Saint Peter upon Cornhill, City of London
Price, John, 20 November 1682, age 16, Talbot County, Maryland,
 Andrew Price

Roberts, Margret, daughter of John and Joan Roberts, Baptized
 12 January 1678/9, Saint Giles in the Fields, Holborn, Camden
Roberts, Margarett, 2 August 1697, age 18, Henrico County, Virginia,
 Edward Haskins

Wilton, John, son of John and Frances Wilton, Baptized 22 July 1691,
 Saint Dunstan in the West, City of London
Welton, John, 18 August 1702, age 10, Talbot County, Maryland,
 Samuell Davis

POSSIBLE MATCHES FROM LONDON

"London, England, Church of England Baptisms, Marriages and Burials, 1538-1812," compiled by London Metropolitan Archives, London, England, https://www.ancestry.com/search/collections/lmaearlyparish/

"England Births and Christenings, 1538-1975," International Genealogical Index, https://familysearch.org/search/collection/igi

"Without Indentures: Index to White Slave Children in Colonial Court Records," Richard Hayes Phillips, Ph.D., Genealogical Publishing Co., 2013.

Brooke, Thomas, son of John Brooke, Baptized 6 March 1664, Saint Giles Cripplegate, City of London
Brooke, Thomas, 10 March 1674, age 11, Charles County, Maryland, John Lambert

Bryan, Thomas, son of Thomas and Elizabeth Bryan, Baptized 16 December 1683, Saint Giles in the Fields, Holborn, Camden
Bryan, Thomas, 20 June 1699, age 16, Talbot County, Maryland, Susanna Harris

Campion, John, son of Thomas and Margaret Campion, Baptized 3 June 1688, Saint John of Wapping, Tower Hamlets, Middlesex
Campin, John, 12 November 1706, age 19, Charles County, Maryland, Ralphaell Neale

Carpenter, Charl(e)s, son of William and Mary Carpenter, Baptized 17 March 1666/7, Saint Olave, Bermondsey, Southwark, Surrey
Carpenter, Charles, 29 December 1680, age 12, Northumberland County, Virginia, Capt. Isaac Foxcroft

Dowell, William, son of William Dowell, Baptized 26 December 1683, Saint Mary, Hendon, Barnet, Middlesex
Dowell, William, 4 May 1695, age 12, Surry County, Virginia, John Hancock, "who came into this Colony this present shipping in the Ship, Hampshire

Gilbert, John, son of Thomas Gilbert, Baptized 23 August 1666, Saint Mary, Ealing, Ealing, Middlesex
Gilbert, John, 9 March 1681, (age 14), Lancaster County, Virginia, William Lennell, ten years

POSSIBLE MATCHES FROM LONDON

Hayes, John, son of Charles and Margarett Hayes, Baptized
    22 October 1689, Saint Alfege, Greenwich, London
Hayes, John, 21 January 1701, age 10, Talbot County, Maryland,
    Rodger Baxter

Holloway, Richard, son of Henry Holloway, Baptized 10 July 1659,
    Saint Saviour, Southwark, Surrey
Holloway, Richard, 9 November 1674, age 14, Accomack County, Virginia,
    Edmund Kelly

James, John, son of Robert and Susan, Baptized 5 June 1645,
    Saint Andrew, Undershaft, City of London
James, John, 12 March 1662, (age 17), Lancaster County, Virginia,
    Thomas Warwicke, seven years

Kent, John, son of Isaac and Francis Kent, Baptized 13 July 1660,
    Saint Botolph, Aldersgate, City of London
Kent, John, 10 May 1676, (age 17), Lancaster County, Virginia,
    Lt. Coll. John Carter, seven years

Kinge, George, son of Thomas and Jane Kinge, Baptized 28 March 1660,
    Saint Anne and Saint Agnes, City of London
King, George, 20 May 1671, age 10, Northumberland County, Virginia,
    Robert Jones

Loyd, William, son of William and Susanah Loyd, Baptized
    25 October 1686, Saint Botolph, Aldersgate, City of London
Lloyd, William, 18 June 1700, age 14, Talbot County, Maryland,
    Nicholas Lowe

Mathewes, John, son of Henrie Mathewes, Baptized 18 March 1648/9,
    Saint Giles, Camberwell, Southwark, Surrey
Mathews, John, 5 January 1664, age 14, Charles County, Maryland,
    John Lewgar

Newman, Anne, daughter of Richard Newman, Baptized 5 October 1651,
    Saint Mary, Battersea, Wandsworth, Surrey
Newman, Ann, 11 January 1670, age 17, Charles County, Maryland,
    William Barton

POSSIBLE MATCHES FROM LONDON

Parker, Ann, daughter of Arthur Parker, Baptized 12 November 1649,
    Saint Saviour, Southwark, Surrey
Parker, Ann, 8 June 1669, age 19, Charles County, Maryland, John Cage

Pearson, John, son of Samuell and Jone Pearson, Baptized
    11 March 1659/60, Saint Leonard, Shoreditch, Hackney, Middlesex
Pearson, John, 11 January 1676, age 17, Charles County, Maryland,
    Raiph Shaw

Roberts, Ann, daughter of John Roberts, Baptized 19 February 1662/3,
    Saint Mary, Willesden, Brent, Middlesex
Roberts, Anne, 8 June 1675, age 11-12, Somerset County, Maryland,
    Samuell Long

Rowland, Francis, son of John and Mary Rowland, Baptized
    17 December 1696, Saint Saviour, Southwark, Surrey
Rowland, Francis, 14 November 1710, age 12, Anne Arundel County,
    Maryland, John Navarr, ten years

Sharpe, Elisabeth, daughter of George and Elisabeth Sharpe, Baptized
    28 June 1686, Saint Ann Blackfriars, City of London
Sharp, Elizabeth, 28 June 1698, age 11, Prince George's County, Maryland,
    William Mills

Waters, John, son of Lancelot and Mary Waters, Baptized 20 July 1684,
    Saint James Garlickhythe, City of London
Waters, John, 14 February 1700, age 15, Lancaster County, Virginia,
    Thomas Martin, nine years

Waters, Robart, son of Robart Waters, Baptized 22 October 1663,
    Saint Mary, Hendon, Barnet, Middlesex
Waters, Robert, 14 January 1678, age 14, York County, Virginia,
    Mathew Edwards, "imported in the Concord, Capt. Thomas
    Grantham, Commander," ten years

Watts, William, son of Richard and Sarah Watts, Baptized 20 June 1683,
    Saint Martin, West Drayton, Hillingdon, Middlesex
Watt (?), William, 1 February 1699, age 15, Henrico County, Virginia,
    ____ Perkins

KIDS FROM ESSEX

"Essex, England, Church of England Baptisms, Marriages, and Burials, 1538-1912," prepared by Essex Record Office, Chelmsford, England, https://www.ancestry.com/search/collections/essexearlyparish/

"Without Indentures: Index to White Slave Children in Colonial Court Records," Richard Hayes Phillips, Ph.D., Genealogical Publishing Co., 2013.

Amis, John, son of Abraham Amis, Baptized 28 September 1651,
    Great Dunmow, Saint Mary the Virgin, Essex, England
Amis, John, 20 June 1668, age 15, Northumberland County, Virginia,
    Col. Peter Ashton

Baxter, Robert, son of Robert and Mary Baxter, Baptized 11 August 1663,
    Wix, Saint Mary, Essex, England [1]
Baxter, Robert, 16 January 1684, age 21, Talbot County, Maryland,'
    Capt. Librey

Bonson (sic), John, son of William and Ann Bonson, Baptized
    26 October 1658, Wickham Saint Paul, All Saints, Essex, England
Benson, John, 14 June 1670, age 11, Charles County, Maryland,
    Mr. Prouce, by Thomas Allanson

Big, Ambrosius, son of Johannis and Mariae Big, Baptized 2 May 1647,
    Elmstead, Saint Anne and Saint Lawrence, Essex, England
Bigs, Ambros, 8 March 1664, age 19, Charles County, Maryland,
    Thomas Baker

Boothe, Richard, son of Thomas and Elizabeth Boothe, Baptized
    31 January 1668, West Ham, All Saints, Essex, England
Booth, Richard, 19 July 1682, age 11, Northumberland County, Virginia,
    Peter Presly, Jr.

---

[1] See also Kids from Cheshire, in *"Birth and Shipping Records"*

KIDS FROM ESSEX

Bourne, John, son of John and Mary Bourne, Baptized 1649,
High Roding, All Saints, Essex, England
Bourne, John, 27 May 1667, age 17 "on the first of August,"
Accomack County, Virginia, Col. Edm. Scarburgh.
"The servants acknowledged these ages."

Bridge, Stephen, son of John and Barbara Bridge, Baptized
6 October 1663, Pebmarsh, Saint John the Baptist, Essex, England
Bridges, Stephen, 9 March 1686, age 25, Charles County, Maryland,
John Court Jun.

Bright, Edward, son of John and Elisabeth Bright, Born 29 March 1667,
Coggeshall, Saint Peter ad Vincula, Essex, England
Bright, Edward, 11 June 1678, age 12, Charles County, Maryland,
James Smallwood

Chambers, Charles, son of Charles and Elizabeth Chambers, Baptized
15 January 1668, South Weald, Saint Peter, Essex, England
Chambers, Charles, 20 June 1682, age 15, Talbot County, Maryland,
Peter Denny

Corbet, Elizabeth, daughter of Thomas and Maria Corbet, Baptized
2 April 1663, West Ham, All Saints, Essex, England
Corbet, Elizabeth, 11 February 1680, (age 14), Lancaster County, Virginia,
William Merriman, ten years

Deaton, Sarah, daughter of John and Mary Deaton, Baptized 5 August 1660,
Dedham, Saint Mary the Virgin, Essex, England
Daton, Sarah, 26 November 1677, age 16, Northampton County, Virginia,
John Eyres

David, James, son of John David, Born 18 February 1656, Wivenhoe,
Saint Mary the Virgin Daton, Essex, England
Davids, James, 19 January 1676, age 17, Northumberland County, Virginia,
Major Thomas Brereton

Dawson, Henry, son of William Dawson, Baptized 23 February 1660,
Barking, Saint Margaret, Essex, England
Dawson, Henry, 27 August 1675, (age 15), Talbot County, Maryland,
William Dunderdell, seven years

KIDS FROM ESSEX

Doman, John, son of William Doman, Born 10 February 1660,
    Coggeshall, Saint Peter ad Vincula, Essex, England
Dowman, John, 2 February 1677, age 18, Accomack County, Virginia,
    Phillip Fisher

Easther, John, son of Saye (sic) Easther, Baptized 14 November 1650,
    Great Dunmow, Saint Mary the Virgin, Essex, England
Easter, John, 9 November 1664, (age 16), Lancaster County, Virginia,
    Alexander Reade, eight years

English, John, son of George and Sarah English, Baptized 3 June 1690
    and 11 June 1690, Wakes Colne, All Saints, Essex, England
English, John, 10 May 1701, age 10, Essex County, Virginia,'
    John Picket

Evored, George, son of George and Mary Evored [spelled "Everet"
    in parents' marriage record – ed.], Baptized 28 April 1672,
    Pentlow, Saint George, Essex, England
Everatt, George, 14 January 1688, age 16, Talbot County, Maryland,
    John Whittington

Gilbert, Jane, daughter of Georgia Gilbert, Baptized 26 January 1668,
    Great Bardfield, Saint Mary the Virgin, Essex, England
Gilbert, Jane, 9 March 1686, age 20, Charles County, Maryland,
    William Hatch

Geble (sic), John, son of Roger and Mary Geble, Baptized 12 May 1661,
    Heydon, Holy Trinity, Essex, England
Goble, John, 9 February 1676, (age 14), Lancaster County, Virginia,
    Thomas Marshall, "who doth give" the servant "two yeres
    of his saide tyme," eight years

Grant, Mary, daughter of Edward Grant, Baptized 30 November 1648,
    Great Parndon, Saint Mary the Virgin, Essex, England
Grant, Mary, 11 January 1665, (age 17), Lancaster County, Virginia,
    William Frizell, seven years

KIDS FROM ESSEX

Gordon, Thomas, son of Georgie Gordon, Baptized 12 April 1653,
    Debden, Saint Mary the Virgin, Essex, England
Gurden, Thomas, 25 January 1669, age 15, York County, Virginia,
    Henry Freeman, nine years

Guy, John, son of John and Mary Guy, Baptized 3 April 1659,
    Chadwell Saint Mary, Saint Mary the Virgin, Essex, England
Guy, John, 9 March 1670, (age 13), Lancaster County, Virginia,
    Robert Griggs, eleven years

Hard (sic), Robert, son of Robert and Mary Hard [spelled "Heard"
    in same parish – ed.], Baptized 15 March 1662,
    Shalford, Saint Andrew, Essex, England
Hurd, Robert, 19 March 1672, age 12, Talbot County, Maryland,
    John Pawsson, ten years

Kent, Robert, son of Robert and Mary Kent, Baptized 2 April 1658,
    Thaxted, Saint John the Baptist, Essex, England
Kent, Robert, 13 April 1669, age 12, Charles County, Maryland,
    John Dent

King, James, son of John and Edith King, Baptized 3 March 1665,
    Great Wigborough, Saint Stephen, Essex, England
King, James, (torn) June 1683, age 19, Talbot County, Maryland,
    John Poore

King, Jane, daughter of John and Jane King, Baptized 1666,
    Sible Hedingham, Saint Peter, Essex, England [2]
King, Jane, 18 March 1684, age 18, Talbot County, Maryland,
    Albert Johnson

Lambert, Edward, son of William and Margaret Lambert, Baptized
    21 May 1673, Little Warley, Saint Peter, Essex, England
Lambert, Edward, 9 May 1688, (age 15), Lancaster County, Virginia,
    William Therriatt, nine years

--------------------------------------- --

[2] See also Kids from Cheshire, in *"Birth and Shipping Records"*

KIDS FROM ESSEX

Lilly, William, son of William and Mary Lilly, Baptized 19 August 1680, Belchamp Otten, Saint Ethelbert and All Saints, Essex, England
Lily, William, 6 June 1694, age 15, Richmond County, Virginia, John Burkett

Mason, Richard, son of John and Elizabeth Mason, Baptized 9 October 1667, Writtle, All Saints, Essex, England
Mason, Richard, 6 March 1676, age 9, Middlesex County, Virginia, Michael Musgrove, "comeing into this Country in ye Shipp, Duke of Yorke"

Morton, Richard, son of John and Isabell Morton, Baptized 6 November 1662, East Tilbury, Saint Catherine, Essex, England
Morton, Richard, 30 May 1676, age 15, Northampton County, Virginia,' Lt. Coll. William Waters

Monke, Elizabeth, daughter of John and Bridget Monke, Baptized 21 November 1644, Waltham Holy Cross, Saint Lawrence and Holy Cross, Essex, England [3]
Mounke, Elisabeth, 10 February 1663, age 18, Charles County, Maryland, John Cherman

Newman, Hannah, daughter of Hannah Newman, Baptized 22 September 1676, Dedham, Saint Mary the Virgin, Essex, England [4]
Newman, Hannah, 12 January 1686, age 11, Charles County, Maryland, Henry Hawkins

Nichols, Robert, son of Daniel and Ann Nichols, Baptized 13 September 1677, Boreham, Saint Andrew, Essex, England [5]
Nichols, Robert, 9 June 1691, age 16, Somerset County, Maryland, Major Robert King, "Came into this County with one Capt. John Jury Comander of the shipp Mary"

---

[3] See also Kids from Gloucester, in *"Birth and Shipping Records"*

[4] See also Kids from Portsmouth, in *"Birth and Shipping Records"*

[5] See also Kids from Cheshire, in *"Birth and Shipping Records"*

KIDS FROM ESSEX

Nun, William, son of William and Eleanor Nun, Baptized 4 November 1667,
Cavering, Saint Mary and Saint Clement, Essex, England
Nonna, William, (torn) 1683, age 16, Talbot County, Maryland,
Bryan Omaly

Pearle, Anne, daughter of Zechcary and Anne Pearle, Baptized
28 December 1686, Willingale Spain, Saint Andrew, Essex, England
Pearle, Anne, 19 January 1699, age 15, Northumberland County, Virginia,
Capt. William Hanson

Potts, John, son of John and Martha Potts, Baptized 25 March 1649,
Thaxted, Saint John the Baptist, Essex, England
Potts, John, 8 June 1686, age 24, Charles County, Maryland,
Capt. Bowling

Reene, Mary, daughter of Richard Reene, Baptized 18 September 1664,
South Weald, Saint Peter, Essex, England
Renes, Mary, 12 June 1688, age 22, Charles County, Maryland,
Mark Lampton, Indenture judged not good "without further proof"

Rust, Robert, son of James and Margarett Rust, Baptized 22 March 1663,
Barnston, Saint Andrew, Essex, England
Rust, Robert, 9 September 1674, (age 12), Lancaster County, Virginia,
George Trott, twelve years

Shaw, Mary, daughter of George and Anne Shaw, Baptized
14 October 1662, Halstead, Saint Andrew, Essex, England
Shaw, Mary, 12 June 1683, age 19, Charles County, Maryland,
Capt. Casheene

Simson, Samuel, son of Thomas and Mary Simson, Baptized 4 April 1660,
Pentlow, Saint George, Essex, England
Simpson, Samuell, 12 August 1673, age 15, Charles County, Maryland,
John Goodge, by Captn. Josias Fendall

KIDS FROM ESSEX

Stille, William, son of William and Jane Stille, Baptized 19 January 1646, White Roding, Saint Martin, Essex, England [6]
Still, William, 20 April 1663, age 16, Charles City County, Virginia, Francis Redford

Tison, Robert, son of William Tison, Baptized 15 October 1665, Barking, Saint Margaret, Essex, England
Tyson, Robert, 15 June 1683, age 18, Accomack County, Virginia, Owen Collonon

Wakefeeld, William, son of John and Juda Wakefeeld, Baptized 2 February 1645, Henham, Saint Mary the Virgin, Essex, England
Wakefield, William, 14 May 1662, (age 18), Lancaster County, Virginia, Rowland Mackrorey, six years

Wale, James, son of George Wale, Baptized 9 November 1687, Burnham-on-Crouch, Saint Mary the Virgin, Essex, England
Wale, James, 14 June 1699, age 12, Lancaster County, Virginia, Coll. Robert Carter, twelve years

Whale, Richard, son of Thomas Whale, Baptized 21 August 1670, Chelmsford, Saint Mary the Virgin, Essex, England
Wayle, Richard, 14 December 1685, age 14, Mrs. Elizabeth Wormeley, "comeing into this Country in ye Shipp, Booth"

---

[6] See also Kids from Scotland, in *"Birth and Shipping Records"*

KIDS FROM WILTSHIRE

"Wiltshire, England, Church of England Baptisms, Marriages and Burials, 1538-1812," Wiltshire and Swindon History Centre, Chippenham, England, https://www.ancestry.com/search/collections/wiltshireearlyparish/

"Without Indentures: Index to White Slave Children in Colonial Court Records," Richard Hayes Phillips, Ph.D., Genealogical Publishing Co., 2013.

Batcheller, Thomas, son of Thomas and Martha Batcheller, Baptized 30 May 1667, Winsley, Wiltshire, England [1]
Batcheller, Thomas, 13 January 1679, age 12, Middlesex County, Virginia, John Sheppard, "comeing into this Country in ye Shipp, Zebulon"

Bisse, Thomas, son of Edward Bisse, Born 28 November 1657, Ashton Keynes, Wiltshire, England
Bissey, Thomas, 7 January 1671, (age 12), Talbot County, Maryland, Henry Willcokes, nine years

Butler, Hugh, son of Bennibimine Butler, Baptized 12 October 1644, Corsham, Wiltshire, England
Buttler, Hugh, 15 March 1663, age 15, Talbot County, Maryland, William Taylor, six years

Cooper, Roger, son of James and Marye Cooper, Baptized 3 April 1663, Upavon, Wiltshire, England
Cooper, Roger, 11 March 1679, age 16, Charles County, Maryland, William Hinsey, by Joseph Bullott

Coussens, Frances, son of Frances Coussens, Born 6 June 1666, Westbury, Wiltshire, England
Cozens, Francis, 24 February 1682, age 14, York County, Virginia, Richard Albritton, "imported in ye Barnaby," Capt. Mathew Rider, Commander

Drew, Jane, daughter of Anthony and Elizabeth Drew, Baptized 4 December 1674, Bishops Canning, Wiltshire, England
Drewe, Jane, 11 August 1691, age 15-18, Somerset County, Maryland, James Sanster

Foster, Michael, son of Michael Foster, Born 8 November 1658, Marlborough, Saint Peter and Saint Paul, Wiltshire, England
Foster, Michell, male, 18 January 1670, (age 10), Talbot County, Maryland, Thomas Heythcott, eleven years

KIDS FROM WILTSHIRE

Gibbs, Anthony, son of Anthony Gibbs, Baptized 14 March 1674/5,
Warminster, Saint Denys with Saint Lawrence, Wiltshire, England
Gibbs, Anthony, 14 January 1688, age 10, Talbot County, Maryland,
Andrew Price

Giles, Edward, son of Edward Giles, Baptized 22 January 1670/1,
Highworth, Wiltshire, England
Giles, Edward, 26 January 1680, age 11, York County, Virginia,
Robert Crawley, "comeing in this yeare in the Richard & Elizabeth,
Capt. Price (?), Commander, in James River"

Giles, John, son of Richard Giles, Baptized 16 August 1691,
Purton with Braydon, Wiltshire, England
Gyles, John, 31 January 1700, age 10, Westmoreland County, Virginia,
John Chilton

Greneway, Elizabeth, daughter of Thomas Greneway, Born 1 July 1659,
Baptized 28 July 1659, Cliffe-Pypard, Wiltshire, England
Greeneway, Elizabeth, 10 January 1677, age 18-22, Somerset County,
Maryland, Ambrose Dixon

Grymes, Edward, son of John and Mary Grimes, Baptized 3 March 1677/8,
Oaksey, Wiltshire, England
Grimes, Edward, 4 April 1694, age 13, Northumberland County, Virginia,
Bartholomew Schreever

Gye, Roger, son of Roger Gye and Mary Musprat, Baptized
23 October 1686, Urchfont, Wiltshire, England
Guy, Roger, 28 February 1700, age 16, Westmoreland County, Virginia,
Francis Self

Hichcox, John, son of Andrew Hichcox, Baptized 5 March 1647/8,
Lacock, Wiltshire, England [2]
Hitchcock, John, 3 May 1660, age 12, Northumberland County, Virginia,
Major George Colclough, nine years

Jacob, Edward, son of Edward and Bridget Jacob, Baptized
15 September 1661, Inglesham, Wiltshire, England
Jacobs, Edward, 20 June 1668, age 9, Northumberland County, Virginia,
Edward Saunders

KIDS FROM WILTSHIRE

James, Robert, son of John James "the first," Baptized 1 March 1659/60,
    Mere, Wiltshire, England
James, Robert, 16 April 1675, age 13, Accomack County, Virginia,
    Daniel Derby

Jefferyes, Thomas, son of Thomas Jefferyes, Baptized 16 December 1660,
    Chippenham Saint Andrew, Wiltshire, England
Jeffreyes, Thomas, 8 March 1681, age 18, Charles County, Maryland,
    Joseph Maninge, by his son in law Mr. Stone

Little, Elizabeth, daughter of James and Eliz: Little, Baptized
    10 November 1661, Chisledon, Wiltshire, England [3]
Little, Elizabeth, 15 June 1675, (age 13), Talbot County, Maryland,
    Petter Deney, nine years

Madox, Edward, son of Richard Madox "the Second," Baptized
    26 October 1653, Kilmington, Saint Mary, Wiltshire, England
Maddox, Edward, 26 April 1670, age 16, York County, Virginia,
    Lt. Col. Daniel Parke, "imported in the Loyall Berkeley"

Muston, Thomas, son of Will Muston, Baptized 21 October 1685,
    Britford, Wiltshire, England
Mustin, Thomas, 1 February 1700, age 13, Westmoreland County, Virginia,
    Andrew Munro

Parrat, Richard, son of Richard and Ane Parrat, Baptized
    12 February 1664/5, Seend, Wiltshire, England [4]
Parrott, Richard, 30 December 1679, age 14 "and two months,"
    Northampton County, Virginia, John Bellamy

Peeters, Margarett, daughter of John and Martha Peeters, Baptized
    11 May 1677, Salisbury, Saint Edmond, Wiltshire, England [5]
Peters, Margrett, 4 April 1694, age 16, Northumberland County, Virginia,
    Mrs. Jane Wildey, eight years

Piper, Richard, son of Nicolas Piper, Baptized 22 September 1661,
    Allington, Wiltshire, England
Piper, Richard, 12 May 1669, (age 9), Lancaster County, Virginia,
    Rawleigh Travers, fifteen years

KIDS FROM WILTSHIRE

Plaire, Henry, son of Robart and Mary Plaire, Born 30 May 1655,
   Bratton, Wiltshire, England
Player, Henry, 25 November 1669, age 15, Northumberland County,
   Virginia, Daniel Neale

Poulter, Charles, son of Charles and Eliz: Poulter, Born 17 March 1656/7,
   Baptized 26 March 1657, Salisbury, Saint Thomas,
   Wiltshire, England
Poulter, Charles, 15 June 1675, (age 14), Talbot County, Maryland,
   William Finey, eight years

Pruet, Beniamin, son of William and Rebecka Pruet, Baptized
   27 March 1670, Saint Martin, Wiltshire, England
Pruitt, Benjamin, 11 May 1686, age 16, Accomack County, Virginia,.
   John Washbourne

Reily, Sarah, daughter of Joseph and Sarah Reily, Baptized 29 July 1667,
   Wilton, Wiltshire, England
Riley, Sarah, 17 April 1678, age 13, Northumberland County, Virginia,
   Daniell Neale

Waters, Beniamin, son of Beniamin and Elianor Waters, Baptized
   9 July 1675, Wilton, Wiltshire, England
Waters, Benjamin, (torn) 1683, age 10, Talbot County, Maryland,
   Bryan Omaly

Wigginton, Georgius (sic), son of Samuilis (sic) and Francisca Wigginton,
   Baptized 18 January 1684/5, Woodborough, Wiltshire, England
Wigginton, George, 20 December 1699, age 15, Northumberland County,
   Virginia, Richard Tullos

---

[1] See also Kids from Scotland, in *"Birth and Shipping Records"*

[2] [3] See also Kids from Gloucester, in *"Birth and Shipping Records"*

[4] [5] See also Kids from Cheshire, in *"Birth and Shipping Records"*

KIDS FROM DORSET

"Dorset, England, Church of England Baptisms, Marriages and Burials, 1538-1812," compiled by Dorset History Centre, Dorchester, England, https://www.ancestry.com/search/collections/dorsetparishregpre1813/

"Without Indentures: Index to White Slave Children in Colonial Court Records," Richard Hayes Phillips, Ph.D., Genealogical Publishing Co., 2013.

Aty, Christopher, son of Christopher Aty, Baptized 24 December 1643, Broadwindsor, Dorset, England
Atty, Christopher, 14 May 1662, (age 18), Lancaster County, Virginia, John Meredith, six years

Bent, Robert, son of Robert Bent, Baptized 5 (?) July 1655, Charmouth, Dorset, England
Bent, Robert, 11 November 1674, (age 16), Lancaster County, Virginia, Robert Beckingham, eight years

Bryent, Daniell, son of Daniell Bryent, Baptized 17 April 1688, Thorncombe, Dorset, England
Bryant, Daniell, 5 June 1699, age 12, Middlesex County, Virginia, Paul Thilman

Bull, William, son of William Bull, Baptized 20 February 1660/1, Bridport, Dorset, England
Bull, William, 10 June 1679, age 18, Charles County, Maryland, John Gooch

Devenish, John, son of Peter Devenish, Baptized 9 February 1650/1, Dorchester, Holy Trinity, Dorset, England
Devenish, John, 16 February 1665, age 13, Accomack County, Virginia, Col. Edm. Scarburgh

Dill, Henry, son of Richard Dill, Baptized 10 October 1655, Morden, Dorset, England
Dill, Henry, 19 July 1680, age 13, Middlesex County, Virginia, Augustine Cant, "comeing into this Country in ye Shipp, Baltemore"

KIDS FROM DORSET

Dunford, William, son of William and Luce Dunford, Baptized 8 June 1658, Toller Porcorum, Wiltshire, England
Dunford, William, 24 March 1675, age 16, York County, Virginia, Bryan Canady, "imported in the Thomas & Edward, Capt. John Martin, Commander," eight years

Ford, Katherine, daughter of Thomas and Grace Ford, Baptized 8 December 1661, Bradford Abbas, Dorset, England
Foard, Katherine, 14 August 1683, age 20, Charles County, Maryland, Phillip Lynes

Gilbert, Henry, son of Henry and Frances Gilbert, *"sed genitus ante legitimum matrimonium,"* Baptized 9 September 1663, Lytchett Matravers, Dorest, England
Gilbert, Henry, 17 April 1677, age 16, Norfolk County, Virginia, Thomas Godby

Hackett, Mary, daughter of Thomas Hackett, Baptized 7 November 1646, Corfe Castle, Dorset, England [1]
Hackitt, Mary, 20 June 1693, age 14 1/2, Accomack County, Virginia, James Gray

Hazzard, James, son of John Hazzard, Baptized 6 January 1660/1, Childe Okeford, Dorset, England
Hazard, James, 15 June 1675, (age 15), Talbot County, Maryland,' Robert Bryon, seven years

Knight, Peter, son of Thomas and Julian Knight, Baptized 21 May 1693, Mapperton, Dorset, England
Knight, Peter, 27 June 1710, age 15, Prince George's County, Maryland, Richard Grrome

Larance (?), James, son of Samuell and Esther Lawrence, Baptized 25 February 1683/4, Seaborough, Dorset, England
Lawrence, James, 4 April 1699, age 17, Charles County, Maryland, James Cotteroll

---

[1] See also Kids from Gloucester, in *"Birth and Shipping Records"*

KIDS FROM DORSET

Larence (sic), Charles, son of John and Ann Larence, Baptized
21 August 1665, Gussage, All Saints, Dorset, England
Lawrance, Charles, 7 January 1678, age 14, Middlesex County, Virginia,
John Wortham, "comeing into this Countrey in the Shipp,
Comard" [Concord – ed.]

Marten, Pettar, son of Samuell and Martha Marten, Baptized
6 March 1689/90, Dorchester, All Saints, Dorset, England [2]
Martin, Peter, 7 May 1700, age 9, Surry County, Virginia,
Edward Morland, "who came into this Countrey this present yeare
in the Shipp, Anne and Mary, Richard Tibbetts, Master"

Pook, Margaret, daughter of Witt and Susanna Pook, Baptized
21 October 1688, Bettiscombe, Dorset, England
Poke, Margrett, 14 November 1710, age 19, Charles County, Maryland,
George Dent

Riddle, Andrew, son of Edward and Ann Riddle, Baptized
14 November 1686, Winterborne Saint Martin, Dorset, England
Riddle, Andrew, 19 March 1700, age 14, Talbot County, Maryland,
Thomas Jackson

Rutter, William, son of Mathew and Mary Rutter, Baptized
8 January 1657/8, Littonm Cheney, Dorset, England [3]
Rutter, William, 16 July 1673, age 15, Northumberland County, Virginia,
Thomas White

Sims, Thomas, son of Henry and Mary Sims, Baptized 19 October 1658,
Powerstock, Dorset, England
Sims, Thomas, 6 February 1673, age 14, Accomack County, Virginia,
Thomas Parramore

Tubb, Thomas, son of Thomas and Edith Tubb, Baptized 19 April 1647,
Steeple, Dorset, England
Tubb, Thomas, 13 April 1669, age 21, Charles County, Maryland,
Zack Wade

---

[2] [3] See also Kids from Cheshire, in *"Birth and Shipping Records"*

KIDS FROM DORSET

Whitt, Samuell, son of Robert Whitt, Baptized 17 September 1665,
  Corfe Castle, Dorset, England
Whitt, Samuell, 14 November 1676, age 11-12, Charles County, Maryland,
  Benjamin Rozer

Whit, Francis, daughter of Marten Whit, Baptized 10 February 1659/60,
  Shillingstone, Dorset, England
Witt, Francis, 15 June 1675, (age 15), Talbot County, Maryland,
  Simon Irons, seven years

Woodman, George, son of George Woodman, Baptized 12 April 1669,
  Netherbury, Dorset, England
Woodman, George, 4 November 1685, age 15, Old Rappahannock County,
  Virginia, James Scott

KIDS FROM SOMERSET

"Somerset, England, Church of England Baptisms, Marriages, and Burials, 1531-1812," compiled by South West Heritage Trust, Taunton, England, https://www.ancestry.com/search/collections/somersetparishearly/

"Without Indentures: Index to White Slave Children in Colonial Court Records," Richard Hayes Phillips, Ph.D., Genealogical Publishing Co., 2013.

Allie, John, son of John and Judith Allie, Baptized 14 April 1667, Keynsham, Somerset, England
Alea, John, (torn) June 1683, age 16, Talbot County, Maryland, William Sharpe

Atkins, Joseph, son of Henry Atkins, Baptized 18 March 1651/2, Chard, Somerset, England
Atkins, Joseph, 20 November 1668, age 15, Northumberland County, Virginia, James Robinson

Blandon, John, son of George Blandon, Baptized 7 August 1653, Chewton Mendip, Somerset, England
Blandon, John, 26 February 1672, age 15, York County, Virginia, Daniell Wyld, "as entrusted with the estate of John Bowler," six years

Braine, Abraham, son of John Braine, Baptized 29 June 1672, Keynsham, Somerset, England
Bran, Abraham, 1 February 1684, age 13, Henrico County, Virginia, John Cox Junr.

Burleigh, Robert, son of Robert and Mary Burleigh, Baptized 30 April 1656, Clatworthy, Somerset, England [1]
Burlee, Robert, 6 July 1674, age 15, Middlesex County, Virginia, Henry Corbin, Esqr.

---

[1] See also Kids from Cheshire, in *"Birth and Shipping Records"*

KIDS FROM SOMERSET

Chester, William, son of William and Jane Chester, Baptized 1 July 1685,
    Wells, Saint Cuthbert, Somerset, England
Chester, William, 6 December 1698, age 14, Accomack County, Virginia,
    Jonathan Owen

Clary, John, son of William Clary, Baptized 15 April 1683,
    Stoke, Saint Michael, Somerset, England
Clary, John, 13 June 1699, age 16, Somerset County, Maryland,
    Francis Alexander

Cole, Joane, daughter of John Cole, Baptized 11 May 1672, North Petherton,
    Somerset, England
Cole, Johanna, 1 March 1686, age 14, Middlesex County, Virginia,
    John Nicholls, "comeing in The Barnaby"

Cundie, Mary, daughter of John and Elizabeth Cundie, Baptized
    13 April 1673, Chilcompton, Saint John the Baptist,
    Somerset, England
Cundey, Mary, 5 December 1687, age 17, Middlesex County, Virginia,
    William Churchill, "comeing into this Country in the Shipp, Ann"

Davis, George, son of George and Elizabeth Davis, Baptized
    4 September 1655, Wells, Saint Cuthbert, Somerset, England
Davis, George, 20 June 1676, age 20, Talbot County, Maryland,
    Robert Bulling, six years

Davis, Georg, son of Nicholas and Elloner Davis, Baptized 6 May 1662,
    Wincanton, Somerset, England
Davis, George, 19 December 1677, age 17, Accomack County, Virginia,
    Edward Revell

Dollen, Richard, son of Richard and Mary Dollen, Baptized 1 April 1684,
    Wrigton, Somerset, England
Dollins, Richard, 21 February 1700, age 15, Northumberland County,
    Virginia, John Dawson

Eson, John, son of Edward Eson, Baptized 15 January 1670/1 (?),
    Emborough, Somerset, England
Eason, John, 11 March 1679, age 11, Charles County, Maryland,
    Capt. Humphrey Warren

KIDS FROM SOMERSET

Foord, Mark, son of John and Shusan Foord, Born 22 March 1661/2,
    Baptized 24 March 1661/2, Wrington, Somerset, England
Ford, Marke, 18 February 1673, (age 10), Talbot County, Maryland,
    John Pitt, twelve years

Frank, Robert, son of Roger and Bredget Frank, Baptized 23 October 1653,
    Porlock, Somerset, England
Frank, Robert, 11 March 1663, "a child," (age 10), Westmoreland County,
    Virginia, John Watts, fourteen years

Gready, John, son of Edward Gready, Baptized 11 May 1692,
    Ashbrittle, Somerset, England
Gredey, John, 7 June 1699, age 8, Richmond County, Virginia,
    Thomas Glascock

Griffin, Robert, son of Thomas and Lucy Griffin, Baptized 24 March 1653/4,
    Bath Abbey, Somerset, England
Griffin, Robert, 7 December 1668, age 16, York County, Virginia,
    Edward Wade, eight years

Homan, William, son of William Homan, Baptized 24 December 1672,
    Crewkerne, Somerset, England
Homan, William, 1 June 1686, age 13, Norfolk County, Virginia,
    Thomas Carding (?)

Joyce, John, son of John Joyce, Baptized 15 August 1675,
    Taunton, Saint Mary, Somerset, England
Joyce, John, 20 April 1687, age 11, Northumberland County, Virginia,
    John Bayley

Kinge, Philop, son of James King, Baptized 4 April 1686,
    Taunton Saint James, Somerset, England
King, Phillip, 31 January 1700, age 14, Westmoreland County, Virginia,
    Thomas Weedon

Macey, Elizabeth, daughter of Sam(u)ell and Mary Macey, Baptized
    July 1692, Frome, Saint John, Somerset, England
Macey, Elizabeth, 18 July 1705, age 16, Northumberland County, Virginia,
    Thomas Gill

KIDS FROM SOMERSET

Morle, Christopher, son of Christopher and Eliza Morle, Baptized
 18 February 1651/2, Norton Fitzwarren, Somerset, England
Morrell, Christopher, 10 June 1673, age 20, Charles County, Maryland,
 Richard Chandler

Mortimer, James, son of John Mortimer, Baptized 6 January 1668/9,
 North Petherton, Somerset, England
Mortemore, James, 18 March 1685, age 16, Northumberland County,
 Virginia, John Coutansheau, Sr.

Newton, Richard, son of Peeter Newton, Baptized 23 March 1682/3,
 Taunton Saint Mary, Somerset, England
Newton, Richard, 9 January 1694, age 14, Charles County, Maryland,
 Capt. Ignatius Causin

Perks, John, son of Rich Perks, Baptized 26 January 1689/90,
 Stoke, Saint Michael, Somerset, England
Pirks, John, 9 June 1702, age 12, Charles County, Maryland,
 Francis Goodrick Junr.

Rogers, Mathew, son of John and Lidiah Rogers, Baptized 22 March 1677/8,
 Frome Saint John, Somerset, England
Rogers, Matthew, 28 November 1693, age 16, Kent County, Maryland,
 Thomas Keane

Rose, Dorothy, daughter of Nicholas Rose, Baptized 7 July 1691,
 North Cadbury, Somerset, England
Rosier, Doroy, female, 22 September 1702, age 12, Kent County, Maryland,
 Daniel Norris

Tony, Samuell, son of William and Lucy Toney, Baptized 21 April 1682,
 Norton, Saint Phillip, Somerset, England
Tony, Samuell, 20 June 1699, age 14, Talbot County, Maryland,
 William Dixon

Toye, William, son of William and Mary (?) Toye, Baptized
 25 August 1688, Wellington, Somerset, England
Toy, William, 9 June 1702, age 14, Charles County, Maryland,
 Ltt. Coll. James Smallwood

KIDS FROM SOMERSET

Walter, George, son of Christopher Walter, Baptized 13 May 1689, Glastonbury, Saint John, Somerset, England
Walter, George, 28 November 1701, age 12 "the first day of February preceding being the time the ship arrived he came into the country in," Northampton County, Virginia, William Bell

Ward, Ann, daughter of Wylliam and Alyse Ward, Baptized 11 March 1646/7, Wraxall, Somerset, England [2]
Ward, Anne, 12 May 1663, age 16, Charles County, Maryland, John Nevill

Warnor, Robert, son of Thomas and Elizabeth Warnor, Baptized 5 April 1686, Chard, Somerset, England
Warner, Robert, 24 September 1696, age 10, York County, Virginia, Thomas Pinchbeck, "imported in the ship, Goulden Lyon, Capt. Ransom, commander"

---

[2] See also Kids from Cheshire, in *"Birth and Shipping Records"*

KIDS FROM IRELAND

"Parish Register of Christ Church Cathedral of Lisburn, Connor Diocese, Baptisms" 1637, 1639-1641, 1643-1646, 1655-1700, (upstream from Belfast), on microfilm at the Public Records Office of Northern Ireland (PRONI).

John son of Charles Cammell of Blavis May ye 9th 1682
Cammell, John, 20 May 1696, age 16, Northumberland County, Virginia, Edward Fielding

Margarett da: of Patrick Conner of Lisb: Octo: ye 5th 1683
Conner, Margrett, 9 August 1698, age 14, Somerset County, Maryland, John Hansett

Roger son of John Kenedy of Lisb: June 6th 1683
Kennaday, Rodger, 22 June 1697, age 14, Kent County, Maryland, Henry Hosier

Daniell son of William McDaniell of Lisburn Febr: 29th 1687/88
Mac Dannell, Danniele, 8 June 1708, age 19, Charles County, Maryland, John Manning

Mary daugh: of Thomas Murphy of Lambey June ye 18th 1679
Murphy, Mary, 12 March 1700, age 22, Charles County, Maryland, Richard Combes

Thomas son of Isack Pluncat of Lisburn Octo: ye 13: 1686
Plunkett, Thomas, 7 July 1697, age 12, Princess Anne County, Virginia, Coll. Anthony Lawson

George son of Thomas Preston of Lisburne Nov: the 2d 1676
Preston, George, 25 September 1693, age 15, York County, Virginia, Samuell Eborne, "imported in the shipp, Edward and Francis, Capt. Thomas Mann, commander"

Nathaniell & Jane children of Samuell Walker of Lisb: July the 15th 1683
Walker, Nathaniel, 17 March 1697, age 13, Northumberland County, Virginia, Cuthbert Spann

KIDS FROM ELSEWHERE

"Cheshire, England, Parish Registers, 1538-1909," compiled by Record Office, Cheshire, England https://www.ancestry.com/search/collections/chesireparishreg/

"Gloucestershire, England, Church of England Baptisms, Marriages and Burials, 1538-1813," compiled by Gloucestershire Archives, Gloucester, England, https://www.ancestry.com/search/collections/gloucbmdearly/

"Kent, England, Church of England Baptisms, Marriages, and Burials, 1538-1914," compiled by Kent Archives Office, Maidstone, England, https://www.ancestry.com/search/collections/kentparish/

"Without Indentures: Index to White Slave Children in Colonial Court Records," Richard Hayes Phillips, Ph.D., Genealogical Publishing Co., 2013.

Graves, Margarett, daughter of William and Frances Graves, Baptized 15 December 1695, Chatham, Saint Mary, Kent, England
Graves, Margarett, 26 August 1712, age 17, Queen Anne's County, Maryland, Edward Hambleton, ordered to serve five years on 26 March 1712

Neale, Arthur, son of William Neale, Baptized 29 May 1683, Berkeley, Gloucester, England
Neale, Arther, 28 June 1698, age 15, Prince George's County, Maryland, Allexander Beall

Upton, Thomas, son of Thomas Upton, Baptized 2 February 1688, Wilmslow, Cheshire, England
Upton, Thomas, 7 June 1699, age 11, Richmond County, Virginia, Francis Thornton

INDICTMENTS FOR KIDNAPPING

"Virginia Colonial Records Project"
Depository: Middlesex County Record Office
https://search.ancestry.com/search/db.aspx?dbid=61473
Keyword: Middlesex

3 October 1643 -- Record that Elizabeth Hamlyn was committed to the House of Correction for taking children in the streets and selling them to be carried off to Virginia.

7 November 1655 -- Recognizances for appearance of Christian Chacrett or Sacrett to answer a charge of inveigling Edward and Anne Furnifull and her infant aboard <u>The Planter</u> for Virginia.

8 November 1655 -- Recognizances for appearance of Thomas Orpitt or Allpitt in the same matter.

10 December 1655 -- Richard Medley to support his son Samuel, being unfit by his cruelty to keep the child.

10 January 1656 -- George Lee committed on a charge of sending the son of Richard Medley to Barbados.

10 January 1656 -- Recognizances of George Lee at al. to produce a certificate from the Governor of Virginia of the safe arrival of Richard Medley's son, his health and place, and a copy of his indentures, or else a certificate of the boy's death.

17 February 1656 -- Margaret Geery ordered committed to prison on a charge of combining to convey Richard Hornold (aged 4) into Virginia.

17 February 1656 -- John Hornold confesses he gave 15 shillings to one Barwick for help in conveying his child to Virginia.

9 July 1656 -- Recognizances for appearance of Edward Yonge to answer complaints of Samuel Gill on suspicion of sending him to Virginia.

4 May 1657 -- Recognizances for Sarah Sharp's appearance to answer charges of having four persons aboard ship for transportation to Barbados and Virginia.

INDICTMENTS FOR KIDNAPPING

20 July 1658 -- Recognizances for appearance of John Sands to answer Robert Pratt for enticing his servants Robert Hownsden and John Overton to Virginia, and attempting the same with his servant Nathaniel Baker.

18 August 1658 -- Recognizances for appearance of Anne Gray to answer for spiriting a 16 year old maid, Bonny, aboard Capt. Fox's ship, for Virginia.

11 May 1660 -- Recognizances for appearance of Abigale Willmott to prefer an indictment against Katherine Mayline for unlawfully transporting Anne Hambleton to Virginia.

7 August 1660 -- Recognizances for appearance of Margery Staples to answer for selling her servant Ann Parker to be a slave in Virginia.

6 August 1661 -- Recognizances for appearance of William Stone to answer for transporting George Creech and Thomas Riddle to Virginia.

11 August 1662 -- Recognizance for appearance of William Sumner to prefer an indictment against Robert Phage for enticing Edmond Gregory, apprentice to Hugh Rogers, to be transported to Virginia.

20 September 1663 -- Recognizances for appearance of William Preston to answer for enticing Richard Wood's apprentice Isaac Bosse aboard the Golden Fortune, bound for Virginia.

30 September 1663 -- Recognizances for appearance of Mary Andrus in the same case as above.

20 January 1665 -- True Bill: Robert Dutch assaulted Ralph Bradshaw and unlawfully conveyed him aboard the Elizabeth and Mary with intent to convey him to Virginia and sell him.

13 January 1670 -- Record of fine on William Haverland for assault on Thomas Stone, with the intent to transport him to Virginia.

29 August 1670 -- Memorandum that Thomas Hensley is on bail for assisting in conveying a boy to Virginia.

10 November 1670 -- True Bill: William Thew assaulted Guilford Slingsby, conveyed him aboard the John of London, and transported him to Virginia with intent to sell him.

INDICTMENTS FOR KIDNAPPING

7 June 1671 -- Record of fine on William Thewe for unlawfully transporting Guilford Slingsby to Virginia.

21 September 1674 -- True Bill: Richard Batt assaulted James Simons and unlawfully conveyed him to The George for transportation to Virginia.

22 September 1674 -- Recognizances for appearance of Richard Batt to answer Thomas Ball for spiriting away his apprentice James Simmons (sic) on The George for Virginia.

9 September 1675 -- True Bill: John Rudd assaulted John Hewlett, transported him to Virginia, and sold him there.

5 February 1676 -- True Bill: Elizabeth Collier assaulted Sarah Price, conveyed her to The Rebecca, and transported her to Virginia.

8 May 1676 -- Recognizances for appearance of John Kent to answer for spiriting of John Cressop aboard a ship to transport him to Virginia.

8 September 1676 -- True Bill: Thomas Gore assulted Edward Meade and conveyed him to The Charles with intent to transport him to Virginia.

2 October 1677 -- True Bill: James Buckle assaulted Hester Lambert and unlawfully conveyed her to The Augustine with intent to transport her to Virginia.

4 October 1677 -- The Calendar refers to a memorandum that James Buckle pleads not guilty to unlawfully conveying Hester Lambert to the Augustine with intent to carry her to Virginia.

8 May 1678 -- True Bill: Katherine Ferrendyne and Charles Lattinoe assaulted Susan Gunn and conveyed her to The Hopewell with intent to transport her to Virginia.

1 December 1678 -- True Bill: John Morris assaulted Thomas Russells, conveyed him aboard The Cambridge, and transported him to Virginia.

9 August 1679 -- True Bill: Sara Tedder assaulted Elizabeth Atkinson and conveyed her aboard a ship with intent to transport her to Virginia.

INDICTMENTS FOR KIDNAPPING

1 September 1680 -- True Bill: Ann Servant assaulted Alice Flax, conveyed her aboard The Elizabeth and Katherine, transported her to Virginia and sold her there.

21 September 1681 -- True Bill: Diana Middleton assaulted Mary Hartley and conveyed her to a Virginia ship with intent to transport her overseas.

21 September 1681 -- True Bill: Diana Middleton assaulted Margaret Towers and carried her aboard a Virginia ship with intent to transport her overseas.

21 October 1682 -- Memorandum of injunction on Alice Lamb to give evidence against "Alce Servant" for selling "Alce Flax" into Virginia.

10 December 1682 -- True Bill: Mathew Trim and Sarah Falconer assaulted Elizabeth Partridge, conveyed her aboard The Indee, transported her to Virginia, and sold her.

25 September 1684 -- True Bill: Jane Price assaulted Richard Jackson and unlawfully put him aboard The Jeofferey with intent to convey him to Virginia.

26 September 1684 -- True Bill: Mary Gwyn and Thomas Black assaulted Alice Deakins and put her aboard The Concord, with intent to transport her to Virginia.

INDEX TO SHIP CAPTAINS

Alexander, Robert, ship not named, Talbot County, 1719

Arnall, Thomas, *Richard & Jane*, York County, 1675

Arnold, Thomas, *Henry & Ann*, Middlesex County, 1676, 1678, 1679
York County, 1678, 1679

Arnold, Thomas, *Jeffryes*, Middlesex County, 1685

Atchison, James, *Oliver of Dublin*, Surry County, 1700
York County, 1701

Backler or Backter, Capt., *Richard*, York County, 1688

Beale, Andrew, *Providence*, Norfolk County, 1687

Bowman, John (?), *Pelican*, York County, 1670, 1671

Bradley, Daniell, *John*, York County, 1683

Bradly, John, ship not named, Surry County, 1682, 1684

Broadhead, William, *America*, Charles County, 1701

Browne, Henry (?), *Loyalty*, Middlesex County, 1699

Brumskill, Capt., *Ruth*, York County, 1691

Cant, William, *Providence of Dublin*, Middlesex County, 1699

Cant, William, *London Merchant*, York County, 1706

Carter, Abraham, *Hope*, Surry County, 1700

Chapman, John, *Sarah & Susannah*, Essex County, 1693

Clements, Bartholomew, *Rose & Crown*, York County, 1680
Surry County, 1681

Clems or Clews, Robert, *Happy Entrance*, York County, 1668

Conoway, Robert, *Richard & Jane*, York County, 1671

Conaway, Robert, *Barnaby*, York County, 1671, 1672

Conoway or Conway, Robert, *Prince*, York County, 1669, 1673, 1676
Middlesex County, 1676

Consett, John, *Mary*, York County, 1679
Middlesex County, 1679, 1680

INDEX TO SHIP CAPTAINS

Cooper, Samuel, *Charles*, York County, 1667

Covell, Richard, *Francis(?)*, York County, 1675

Creeke, Henry, *Phillipp*, York County, 1668

Creeke, Henry, *Hercules*, York County, 1673

Creeke, Henry, *Hannah*, Middlesex County, 1676, 1678

Crookshanks, Andrew, *Katherine of London Derry*, Somerset County, 1692

Dell, Capt., *John & William*, Surry County, 1685

Dermott, Terrence, ship not named, Northampton County, 1683

Drew, Roger, *Bristol Factor*, Middlesex County, 1679

Dudley, Robert, *Expectations Briganteene*, Middlesex County, 1700

Edgate or Edgett, Henry, *Endeavor*, York County, 1679

Edwards, Phillip, *Ewe & Lamb*, York County, 1667

Edwards, Phillip (?), *Diamond*, York County, 1680

Ellis, Samuell, *Dove*, Northumberland County, 1706

Ells, Ellis, *Planters Adventure*, York County, 1675, 1676
   Middlesex County, 1676

Elzey, Arnold, *Montgomery*, Somerset County, 1725

Evoling, Christopher, *Rebecca*, York County, 1671, 1673

Faucett, Thomas, *James (Frigatt)*, York County, 1673

Fletcher, William, *Vine*, Essex County, 1695

Ginge or Ginges, Sebastian, *Stephen & Edward*,
   Middlesex County, 1683, 1684, 1685, 1686, 1689

Goar, John, *John Baptist*, Essex County, 1701

Grantham, Thomas, *George*, York County, 1675

Grantham, Thomas, *Concord*, 1675, 1676, 1678, 1679, 1680
   Middlesex County, 1678

Greene, Thomas (?), *John & Martha (?)*, York County, 1671

INDEX TO SHIP CAPTAINS

Groves, Thomas, *John*, York County, 1681
    Surry County, 1681

Gutteridge, Nicholas, *Zebulon*, Middlesex County, 1678, 1679, 1680, 1683

Hall, William, *Providence of London*, Lancaster County, 1664

Harris, John, *James & Benjamin*, Somerset County, 1693

Hasted, Thomas, *Recovery*, Middlesex County, 1678

Hasted, Thomas, *Recovery*, Middlesex County, 1685

Hazelwood, John, *Golden Lyon*, York County, 1684

Hide, Phineas, *Industry*, York County, 1672, 1674

Hilson, John, *Friends Encrease*, York County, 1679

Hobbs, Richard, *Elizabeth & Mary*, York County, 1665

Hobbs, Richard, *Elizabeth*, York County, 1669

Hobbs, Robert, *Elizabeth*, York County, 1668

Hopkins, William, *Loyallty*, Baltimore County, 1684

Jackson, Rowland, *Mayflower*, Somerset County, 1694

James, Thomas, *Duke of Yorke*, Lancaster County, 1664
    York County, 1668

Janson, Capt., *Harridge Prize*, York County, 1700

Jefferys or Jeffreys, William, *Golden Fortune*, York County, 1678, 1679
    Middlesex County, 1678

Jeffreys, William, *Sarah*, York County, 1693, 1701
    Middlesex County, 1696

Jeffreys, James, *Mary*, Somerset County, 1708

Johnson, Frederick, *Elizabeth & Mary*, Surry County, 1697

Jones, William, *Expectation*, Surry County, 1692

Jury, John, *Mary*, Somerset County, 1691

Kelsick, Richard, *Resolution*, Essex County, 1693

INDEX TO SHIP CAPTAINS

Larimore, Thomas, *Rebecca*, Charles City County, 1677

Larimore, Thomas, *Speedwell*, Surry County, 1678

Lashbrooke, Thomas, *Fisher of Biddeford*, Somerset County, 1699

Laycock, Richard, *Susanna*, Middlesex County, 1690

Leach, Joseph, *Sarah of Bristol*, York County, 1692

Lindow, James, *John of Dublin*, Somerset County, 1725

Lindow, James, *Manocan*, Somerset County, 1727

Loch, John, ship not named, Anne Arundel County, 1701

Lows, Edward, *St. Turin*, Somerset County, 1727

Lucam or Lucan, John, *Canary Bird*, York County, 1675

Mann, Thomas, *Edward & Francis*, York County, 1693

Marshall, Thomas, *Sarah*, Kent County, 1701

Martin, John, *Thomas & Edward*, York County, 1673, 1674, 1675

Martin, John, *Friends Encrease*, Middlesex County, 1676
York County, 1676, 1677, 1678

Martin or Martyn, John, *Humphrey & Elizabeth*, York County, 1683

Mecoy, William, *Providence of London*, Somerset County, 1692

Medford, Robert (?), *Humphrey & Elizabeth*, York County, 1674

Moore, John (?), *Post Horse*, York County, 1669, 1671

Morgan, James, *Perry & Lane*, Surry County, 1700

Moseley, William, *Antelope of Belfast*, York County, 1679

Orton, William, ship not named, Surry County, 1685

Pagan, Peter, *Booth*, Middlesex County, 1685

Parsons, Francis, *Paradise*, York County, 1684

Parsons, Francis, *Sarah*, York County, 1689

Peacock, Joseph, *Byrd*, Charles City County, 1694

Pearce, Jeremiah, *James & Mary of Bristoll*, Somerset County, 1699

INDEX TO SHIP CAPTAINS

Peirce, Edward, *Golden Fortune*, York County, 1674

Pensax, Samuel, *Marigold*, Lancaster County, 1665

Picks, Josias, *York Merchant*, York County, 1671

Plover, John (?), *Isaac & Benjamin*, York County, 1671

Prinn or Prynne, Nicholas, *Richard & Elizabeth*, York County, 1680

Purvis, George, *Releife*, Middlesex County, 1677, 1678

Purvis, George, *Baltimore*, Middlesex County, 1679

Purvis, George, *Duke of Yorke*, Middlesex County, 1685, 1686

Purvis, George, *White Fox*, Middlesex County, 1686

Purvis, John, *Duke of Yorke*, Middlesex County, 1676, 1678, 1679, 1680

Ransom, Capt., *Golden Lyon*, York County, 1696

Ranson, Robert, *Planters Adventure*, York County, 1678, 1679 Middlesex County, 1678

Rhodes, Edward, *Constant Mary*, Middlesex County, 1678, 1679 York County, 1681, 1682

Rider, Mathew, *Barnaby*, York County, 1674, 1676, 1679, 1682, Middlesex County, 1686

Rock, William, *Diamond*, Kent County, 1716

Sargeant, Stephen, "a sloop from Jamaica," Somerset County, 1692

Sinners, Capt., *Tryall*, Somerset County, 1733

Smyth, Thomas, *William & Mary*, York County, 1673

Smith (Smyth), Thomas, *Leghorne Merchant*, Middlesex County, 1676 Northumberland County, 1678

Smith, Thomas, *Constant*, York County, 1679

Speding, Lanslott, *Speedwell*, Somerset County, 1723

Spry, Lewis, *Recovery*, Middlesex County, 1686

Stringer, Thomas, *Elizabeth & Mary*, Surry County, 1703

Sutton, Henry, *St. Thomas of London*, Middlesex County, 1691

INDEX TO SHIP CAPTAINS

Symonds, Robert, *Truelove*, York County, 1674

Taylor, Zachary or Zacharias, *Augustine*
York County, 1672, 1676, 1678, 1680, 1681, 1685
Middlesex County, 1680

Tenth, John, *Edward & Sarah*, Dorchester County, 1691

Thomas, John, *Lamb*, Essex County, 1697

Thornton, William, *Jane*, Northumberland County, 1700

Tibbets, Richard, *Anne & Mary*, Surry County, 1699, 1700

Trigany, Henry, *Brothers Adventure*, Surry County, 1684

Trim, Mathew, *Judith*, York County, 1684

Trim, Mathew, *Indy*, York County, 1686

Trimm, Mathew, *Robert & Samuell*, York County, 1698
Middlesex County, 1698

Vanfleeten, John, *Stadt of Staden*, York County, 1674

Varbell, Thomas, *Elizabeth & Mary*, York County, 1658

Videll, John, *John of Dublin*, Somerset County, 1724

Warner, John, *Francis*, York County, 1674

Warren, Thomas, *Daniel (Daniell)*, York County, 1673, 1674

Webber, Leon., *Golden Lyon*, York County, 1674

Wheelock, Abraham (?), *Martha*, York County, 1671

Whiteside, Mr., *Ruby of White Haven*, Somerset County, 1697

Wilkings, Amos (?), *Lady Frances*, Middlesex County, 1676

Willis, Richard, *Vyne of Dublin*, Middlesex County, 1693

Wise, Abraham, *Mary*, York County, 1672

Yoe, John, *Adventure of Biddeford*, Kent County, 1701

Young, Anthony, *James (Frigatt)*, York County, 1680

INDEX TO SHIP ARRIVALS

Abraham & Sarah, Middlesex County, 1676, master not named

Adventure of Biddeford, Kent County, 1701, John Yoe Commander

America, Charles County, 1701, William Broadhead, Master

Ann, Middlesex County, 1687, master not named

Anne & Mary, Surry County, 1699, 1700, Richard Tibbets Master

Antelope of Belfast, York County, 1679, William Moseley, Master

Augustine, York County, 1672, 1676, 1678, 1680, 1681, 1685
    1672, Zachary Taylor, Master
    1676, Capt. Zacarias Taylor Commander
    1678, 1679, Capt. Zachary Taylor Commander
    1680, 1681, 1685, Zachary Taylor (?), Master
Augustine, Middlesex County, 1680, Zacharias Taylor, Master

Baltimore, Middlesex County, 1679, George Purvis, Master
Baltimore, Middlesex County, 1680, master not named

Barnaby, York County, 1671, 1672, 1674, 1676, 1679, 1681, 1682
    1671, 1672, Robert Conaway, Master
    1674, 1676, 1679, 1682, Capt. Matthew Rider, Commander
    1681, Mathew Rider, Master
Barnaby, Middlesex County, 1686, Mathew Rider (?), Master

Booth, Middlesex County, 1685, Peter Pagan, Captain

Bristol Factor, Middlesex County, 1679, Roger Drew, Master

Brothers Adventure, Surry County, 1684, Henry Trigany Master

Byrd, Charles City County, 1694, Joseph Peacock, Master

Canary Bird, York County, 1675, John Lucam or Lucan, Commander

Charles, York County, 1667, Samuel Cooper, Master

58

INDEX TO SHIP ARRIVALS

Cheer, York County, 1700, master not named

Concord, York County 1675, 1676, 1678, 1679, 1680
    Capt. Thomas Grantham Commander
Concord (?), Middlesex County, 1678, [Thomas Grantham]

Constance, York County, 1671, master not named

Constant, York County, 1679, Capt. Thomas Smith Commander

Constant Mary, Middlesex County, 1678, 1679, Edward Rhodes, Master
Constant Mary, York County, 1681, 1682, Capt. Edward Rhodes Commander

Daniel (Daniell), York County, 1671, 1673, 1674
    1671, master not named
    1673, 1674, Capt. Thomas Warren Commander

Diamond, York County, 1680, Capt. Phillip (?) Edwards Commander
    1681, 1682, master not named

Diamond, Kent County, 1716, William Rock, Master

Dove, Northumberland County, 1706, Samuell Ellis, Master

Duke of Yorke, Lancaster County, 1664, Thomas James, Master
Duke of Yorke, York County, 1668, Thomas James, Master
Duke of Yorke, Middlesex County, 1676, 1678, 1679, 1680,
    John Purvis, Master
Duke of Yorke, Middlesex County, 1685, 1686, George Purvis, Master

Edward & Francis, York County, 1693, Capt. Thomas Mann Commander

Edward & Sarah, Dorchester County, 1691, John Tenth Master

Elizabeth, York County, 1668, 1669
    1668, Capt. Robert Hobbs Commander
    1669, Captain Richard Hobbs, Master

INDEX TO SHIP ARRIVALS

Elizabeth & Mary, York County, 1658, Capt. Thomas Varbell,
   1665, Capt. Richard Hobbs Commander
Elizabeth & Mary, Surry County, 1697, Frederick Johnson Commander
   1703, Thomas Stringer Master

Endeavor, York County, 1679, Henry Edgate or Edgett Commander

Expectation, Surry County, 1692, William Jones, Master

Ewe & Lamb, York County, 1667, Philip Edwards, Master

Expectations Briganteene, Middlesex County, 1700, Major Robert Dudley

Fisher of Biddeford, Somerset County, 1699, Thomas Lashbrooke
   Commander

Francis, York County, 1674, John Warner Commander
Francis (?), York County, 1675, Richard Covell, Master

Friends Encrease, Middlesex County, 1676, [John Martin]
Friends Encrease, York County, 1676, 1677, 1678, 1679
   1676, 1677, 1678, Capt. John Martin Commander
   1679, John Hilson Commander

George, York County, 1675, Capt. Thomas Grantham Commander

George of Belfast, Middlesex County, 1687, master not named

George of Bristoll, Middlesex County, 1678, master not named

Golden Fortune, York County, 1674, 1678, 1679
   1674, Capt. Edward Peirce Commander
   1678, 1679, Capt. William Jeffreys Commander
Golden Fortune, Middlesex County, 1678, William Jefferys, Master

Golden Lyon, York County, 1674, 1684, 1696
   1674, Capt. Leon. Webber Commander
   1684, John Hazelwood, Captain
   1696, Capt. Ransom Commander
Golden Lyon, Middlesex County, 1686, master not named

60

INDEX TO SHIP ARRIVALS

Hampshire, Surry County, 1695, master not named

Hannah, Middlesex County, 1676, 1678, Henry Creeke, Master
Hannah, Middlesex County, 1680, master not named

Happy Entrance, York County, 1668, Capt. Robert Clems or Clews, Commander

Harridge Prize, York County, 1700, Capt. Janson Commander

Henry & Ann, Middlesex County, 1676, 1678, 1679, Thomas Arnold, Master
Henry & Ann (Anne), York County, 1678, 1679
    1678, Capt. Thomas Arnold Commander
    1679, Capt. Thomas Arnold Commander

Hercules, York County, 1673, Capt. Henry Creeke Commander

Hope, Surry County, 1700, Abraham Carter Master

Howard, York County, 1680, master not named

Humphrey & Elizabeth, York County, 1674, 1683
    1674, Robert Medford (?), Master
    1683, Capt. John Martin or Martyn Commander

Industry, York County, 1672, 1674
    1672, Phineas Hide, Master
    1674, Capt. Phineas Hide Commander
Industry, Middlesex County, 1678, master not named

Indy, York County, 1686, Capt. Mathew Trim, Commander

Isaac & Benjamin, York County, 1671, John Plover (?), Master

James (Frigatt), York County, 1673, 1680
    1673, Capt. Thomas Faucett Commander
    1680, Capt. Anthony Young Commander

James & Benjamin, Somerset County, 1693, John Harris, Master

James & Mary of Bristoll, Somerset County, 1699, Jeremiah Pearce or Peirce Commander

INDEX TO SHIP ARRIVALS

Jane, Northumberland County, 1700, William Thornton, Master

Jane Kitch from Scotland, York County, 1680, master not named

Jeffryes, Middlesex County, 1685, Thomas Arnold, Master

John & William, Surry County, 1685, Capt. Dell Master

John, York County, 1681, 1683
    1681, Thomas Groves Commander
    1683, Daniell Bradley Master

John & Martha (?), York County, 1671, Thomas Greene (?)

John & Mary, York County, 1668, master not named

John Baptist, Essex County, 1701, John Goar Commander

John of Bridgwater, Middlesex County, 1676, master not named

John of Dublin, Somerset County, 1724, 1725
    1724, John Videll Master
    1725, Capt. James Lindow

Jonathan of Topsham, York County, 1681, master not named

Judith, York County, 1684, Capt. Mathew Trim Commander

Katharine of New Haven, Surry County, 1704, master not named

Katherine of London Derry, Somerset County, 1692, Andrew Crookshanks Master

Lady Frances, Middlesex County, 1676, Amos Wilkings (?), Master

Lamb, Essex County, 1697, John Thomas, Commander

Leghorne Merchant, Middlesex County, 1676, Thomas Smith, Master
Leghorne Merchant, Northumberland County, 1678, Thomas Smith, Master

INDEX TO SHIP ARRIVALS

Leonard & James, Middlesex County, 1679, master not named
Leonard & James, York County, 1679, master not named

London Merchant, York County, 1706, Capt. William Cant Commander

Lovers (sic) *Increase*, York County, 1682, master not named

Loving Friendship, Middlesex County, 1681, master not named

Loyal Berkeley, York County, 1670, master not named

Loyallty, Baltimore County, 1684, William Hopkins
Loyalty, Middlesex County, 1699, Henry Browne (?)

Manocan, Somerset County, 1727, James Lindow Commander

Marigold, Lancaster County, 1665, Samuel Penzax, Master

Martha, York County, 1671, Abraham Wheelock (?), Master

Mary, York County, 1672, Abraham Wise, Master
Mary, York County, 1679, John Consett, Master
Mary, Middlesex County, 1679, 1680, John Consett, Master
Mary, Somerset County, 1691, 1708
    1691, Capt. John Jury Commander
    1708, James Jeffreys Commander

Mayflower, Somerset County, 1694, Rowland Jackson Commander

Montgomery, Somerset County, 1725, Coll. Arnold Elzey

Oake, Middlesex County, 1696, master not named

Oliver, Surry County, 1700, James Atchison or Achison Master
Oliver of Dublin, York County, 1701, Capt. Thomas Adkinson Commander

Owners Advice (sic), Middlesex County, 1679, master not named

Paradise, Middlesex County, 1681, master not named
Paradise, York County, 1684, Francis Parsons Commander

INDEX TO SHIP ARRIVALS

Pelican, York County, 1670, 1671, John Bowman (?), Master

Perry & Lane, Surry County, 1700, James Morgan Master

Phillipp, York County, 1668, Mr. Henry Creeke Commander

Planters Adventure, York County, 1675, 1676, 1678, 1679, 1680, 1681
    1675, Ellis Ellis, Master
    1676, Capt. Ellis Ells or Elias Ellies, Commander
    1678, 1679, Capt. Robert Ranson, Commander
    1680, 1681, master not named
Planters Adventure, Middlesex County, 1676 [Ellis Ells]
Planters Adventure, Middlesex County, 1678 [Robert Ranson]

Post Horse, York County, 1669, 1671, John Moore (?), Master

Prince, York County, 1669, 1673, 1676, 1680, 1681
    1669, Robert Conway, Master
    1673, 1676, Capt. Robert Conoway Commander
    1680, 1681, master not named
Prince, Middlesex County, 1676, [Robert Conoway]

Providence, Norfolk County, 1687, Capt. Andrew Beale Master

Providence of Dublin, Middlesex County, 1699, William Cant, Master

Providence of London, Lancaster County, 1664, William Hall, Commander
Providence of London (?), Northampton County, 1685, Col. John Custis (?)
Providence of London, Somerset County, 1692, William Mecoy Master

Rainbow of Plymouth, Lancaster County, 1664, master not named

Rebecca, York County, 1671, 1673, Capt. Christopher Evoling Commander
Rebecca, Charles City County, 1677, Thomas Larrimore, Commander

Recovery, Middlesex County, 1678, Thomas Hasted, Master
Recovery, Middlesex County, 1680, 1681, master not named
Recovery, Middlesex County, 1685, Thomas Hasted Master
Recovery, Middlesex County, 1686, Lewis Spry, Master

INDEX TO SHIP ARRIVALS

Releife, Middlesex County, 1677, 1678, George Purvis, Master
Releife, Middlesex County, 1685, master not named

Resolution, Essex County, 1693, Richard Kelsick Commander

Resolution of White Haven, Middlesex County, 1689, master not named

Richard, York County, 1688, Capt. Backler or Backter Commander

Richard & Elizabeth, York County, 1680, Nicholas Prinn or Prynne, Commander

Richard & James (sic), York County, 1670, master not named
Richard & Jane, York County, 1671, 1675
    1671, Capt. Robert Conoway Commander
    1675, Capt. Thomas Arnall Commander

Robert & Samuell, York County, 1698, Capt. Mathew Trimm Commander
Robert & Samuell, Middlesex County, 1698, [Mathew Trimm]

Rose & Crown, York County, 1680, Bartholomew Clements Commander

Ruby of White Haven, Somerset County, 1697, Mr. Whiteside, Master
Ruby, 220 tons, Mr. Whiteside Master, at Whitehaven, 1699, 1702, 1709

Ruth, York County, 1691, Capt. Brumskill Commander

St. Thomas of London, Middlesex County, 1691, Henry Sutton, Master

St. Turin, Somerset County, 1727, Edward Lows Commander

Sarah, York County, 1689, 1693, 1701
    1689, Capt. Francis Parsons Commander
    1693, 1701, Capt. William Jeffreys Commander
Sarah of Bristol, York County, 1692, Capt. Joseph Leach Commander
Sarah, Middlesex County, 1696, Wiliam Jeffreys Commander
Sarah, Kent County, 1701, Thomas Marshall Commander

Sarah & Susannah, Essex County, 1693, John Chapman Commander

INDEX TO SHIP ARRIVALS

Speedwell, Surry County, 1678, Thomas Larimore, Master

Speedwell, Somerset County, 1723, Capt. Lanslott Speding Commander

Speedwell of London, Middlesex County, 1691, master not named

Stadt of Staden, York County, 1674, John Vanfleeten Commander

Stephen & Edward, Middlesex County, 1683, 1684, 1685, 1686, 1689
    1683, 1684, 1685, 1686, Sebastian Ginge or Ginges, Master
    1689, Sebastian Gringee, Master

Susanna, Middlesex County, 1690, Richard Laycock, Master

Thomas & Ann, Middlesex County, 1679, master not named

Thomas & Edward, York County, 1673, 1674, 1675
    Capt. John Martin Commander

Truelove, York County, 1674, Robert Symonds, Master

Tryall, Somerset County, 1733, Capt. Sinners Commander

Tryall of Bristol, York County, 1670, master not named

Vine, Essex County, 1695, William Fletcher Commander

Vyne of Dublin, Middlesex County, 1693, Capt. Richard Willis

White Fox, Middlesex County, 1686, George Purvis, Master

William & John, Middlesex County, 1696, master not named

William & Mary, York County, 1673, Capt. Thomas Smyth Commander

York Merchant, York County, 1671, Josias Picks, Master

Zebulon, Middlesex County, 1678, Nich. Gutteridge, Master
Zebulon, Middlesex County, 1679, Nico. Goodridge or Gutheridge, Master
Zebulon, Middlesex County, 1680, 1683, Nicholas Guttridge (?), Master

INDEX TO REVOLUTIONARIES

FLETCHER, CHARLES, Born 26 November 1754, Acton MA. Married 6 June 1780 at Chelmsford MA to Sarah Fletcher. Son of Major Daniel Fletcher and Sarah Hartwell, grandson of Lieut. Jonathan Hartwell and Sarah Wheeler, great-grandson of THOMAS WHEELER SR. and Sarah Davis. Soldiers and Sailors, Vol. 5, Page 770. 19 April 1775.

FLINT, EPHRAIM JR., Born 13 May 1745, Concord MA. Married Catherine Fox, 2 July 1772, Lincoln MA. Died 1 September 1824, Lincoln MA. Son of Ephraim Flint Sr. and Ruth Wheeler, grandson of Thomas Wheeler Jr. and Mary Brooks, great-grandson of THOMAS WHEELER SR. and Sarah Davis. Soldiers and Sailors, Vol. 5, Page 794.

FLINT, JOHN, Born 9 June 1754, Lincoln MA. Married Esther Fuller, 26 July 1795, Lincoln MA. Son of Ephraim Flint Sr. and Ruth Wheeler, grandson of Thomas Wheeler Jr. and Mary Brooks, great-grandson of THOMAS WHEELER SR. and Sarah Davis. Soldiers and Sailors, Vol. 5, Page 797.

HAGER, WILLIAM, Born 25 October 1740, Waltham MA. Son of Joseph Hagar and Grace Biglow, grandson of WILLIAM HAGAR and Sarah Benjamin. Soldiers and Sailors, Vol. 7, Page 27.

HEALD, DANIEL, Born 14 July 1739, Concord MA, Died 17 September 1833, Chester VT. Married 25 December 1760 at Lincoln MA to Abigail Wheeler, daughter of Thomas Wheeler Jr. and Mary Brooks, granddaughter of THOMAS WHEELER SR. and Sarah Davis. Soldiers and Sailors, Vol. 7, Page 653. SAR file #35700. 19 April 1775.

HUDSON, THOMAS, Baptized 1 April 1753, Framingham MA. Son of William Hudson and Dorcas Walkup, grandson of THOMAS WALKUP SR. and Hannah his wife. Enlisted at Reading. Soldiers and Sailors, Vol. 8, Page 462. Fifer, 19 April 1775.

MILLET, DANIEL, Born 1 December 1750, Gloucester MA. Son of Joseph Millett and Elisabeth Abrams, grandson of Bethiah Day and Andrew Millett, great-grandson of JOHN DAY and Abigail Leach. Soldiers and Sailors, Vol. 10, Page 781.

SHIP ARRIVALS IN PHILADELPHIA

9 December 1682	***Antelope of Belfast***, Edward Cooke Master [1]
20 November 1683	Morning Starr of Leverpoole, Thomas Hayes Master
20 March 1686	***Jeffries of London***, Thomas Arnold Master
28 January 1688	***Margeret of London***, John Bowman Commander
22 September 1683	***Elizabeth & Mary***, John Bowman Master
29 September 1683	Endeavour of London, George Thorp Master
6 October 1683	***Concord of London***, William Jefferies Commander [2]
	Providence of Scarbrough, Robert Hopper Master
17 September 1684	Vine of Leverpoole, William Preeson Master, from Dolyserne near Dolgellau in Merionethshire
29 September 1683	***Providence of London***, Robert Hopper Commander
28 September 1683	Bristoll Comfort, John Read Master
1 October 1683	Comfort of Bristol, Captain Reed
31 October 1683	Unicorne of Bristol, Thomas Cooper Master
14 October 1683	Lion of Leverpoole
31 October 1685	Rebecca of Liverpoole, James Skinner Commander
10 November 1685	Bristoll Merchant, John Stephens Commander
29 September 1682	Elizabeth, Ann & Catherine, Thomas Hudson Commander
6 August 1685	***Charles of London***, Edmund Payne Commander
16 October 1685	Francis & Dorothy of London, Richard Bridgeman Commander
16 December 1685	Unicorne of Bristoll, Thomas Cooper Commander
23 June 1686	Desire of Plymouth, James Cook Commander
20 August 1683	America of London, Joseph Wasey Master
c. 31 October 1682	Wellcome of London, Rob Greenway Master
11 July 1686	Delaware of Bristol, John Moore Commander
15 July 1686	Amity of London, Richard Dymond Master

---

[1] Antelope of Belfast, Captain Edward Cook, arrived in Philadelphia from Ireland with 7 emigrants on 9 October 1682., ref. Dobson, David, *"Ships from Ireland to Early America, 1623-1850."* [2] Ship named in Letter from James Claypoole to William Penn, 1 April 1683, London, reprinted in Soderland, Jean R., *"William Penn and the Founding of Pennsylvania, 1680-1684, A Documentary History,"* University of Pennsylvania Press, Philadelphia, 1983, p. 210.

COURT RECORDS, CHESTER COUNTY

"Records of the Courts of Chester County, Pennsylvania, Volume 1, 1681-1697, and Volume 2, 1697-1710," Transcribed by Miss Dorothy B. Lapp and Miss Francis B. Dunlap, Under the Auspices of the Chester County Historical Society, West Chester, Pennsylvania, Published by Richard T. and Mildred C. Williams, Danboro, Pennsylvania, 1972

https://search.ancestry.com/search/db.aspx?dbid=10698

INITIAL COURT APPEARANCES

Allen, Elizabeth, servant to John Wood, 5 October 1697, age not adjudged, five years servitude

Beackly, Adam, servant to David Meredith, 14 September 1697, age 13, eight years servitude

Bean, Ann, servant to Francis Chadsey, 5 October 1697, age not adjudged, five years servitude

Bloustowne, George, servant to Willam Davis, 14 December 1697, (age 13), "seven years and a half" servitude, eight years if taught to read and write, "from the fourteenth day of the seventh month last past"

Breezer, John, servant to David Phillips, 14 December 1697, (age 13), eight years servitude "from the fourteenth day of September last past"

Bruise, William, servant to William Woodmansee, 9 September 1696, (age 13), eight years servitude "from the 20th Day of June last past"

Bruiss, James, servant to John Baldwin, 14 September 1697, age 11, ten years servitude

Bullen, Thomas, servant to Henery Worlye, 9 June 1696, (age 14), seven years servitude

Canide, James, "that Mauris Trent Brought In to this Country," servant to William Collett, 3 October 1693, age 14, seven years servitude

Chambers, Margret, servant to Robert Carter, 9 June 1696, (age 15 1/2), "five yeares and a halfe" servitude "from the 20th Day of May last past"

COURT RECORDS, CHESTER COUNTY

Clowney, William, servant to John Redmeall, 5 October 1697, age 10, ten years servitude, eleven years if taught to read and write, "from the 14th day of September last"

Conner, Margaret, servant to Justice (Jasper) Yeates, 14 September 1697, age not adjudged, five years servitude

Cormutt, Daniel, servant to James Hendricson, 14 September 1697, age 12, nine years servitude

Cuningham, John, servant to John Worrell, 10 March 1696, (age 13), eight years servitude

Davidson, John, servant to John Pennell, 14 December 1697, age 11, nine years servitude, ten years if taught to read and write

Dobie, Lydias, male, servant to Jasper Yeates, 10 March 1696, (age 15), six years servitude

Doell, Emmole, female, servant to James Lowens, 14 September 1697, age not adjudged, five years servitude

Driver, James, "that Mauris Trent Brought In to this Country," servant to William Collett, 3 October 1693, age 14, seven years servitude

Dugles, Isabella, servant to John Ditton, 14 December 1697, age not adjudged, five years servitude "she having been very sick"

Finley, Margaret, servant to John Sharpley, 14 September 1697, age 13, eight years servitude

Flatt, Robert, "brought In by Maurice Trent," servant to Maurice Trent, 1 October 1695, (age 13), eight years servitude

Fraisor, Andrew, "brought In by Maurice Trent," servant to Francis Baldwin, 1 October 1695, age not adjudged, five years servitude

Freezell, Alexander, servant to William Thomas, 14 December 1697, (age 14), "six years and a half" servitude, seven years if taught to read and write, "from the fourteenth day of September last"

Gibb, Robert, servant to Jeremiah Jarman, 14 December 1697, (age 10), eleven years servitude, "from the 14th day of September last past"

COURT RECORDS, CHESTER COUNTY

Gorden, Jeane, female, servant to William Browne, 9 June 1696, age not adjudged, five years servitude

Greenwater, John, servant to Richard Miles, 14 December 1697, (age 13), "seven years & a halfe" servitude, eight years if taught to read and write, "from the 14th day of September last past"

Greeve, George, servant to Edward Joans, 14 September 1697, age 13, eight years servitude

Harper, Thomas, servant to William Cope, 5 October 1697, age not adjudged, five years servitude, "five years and three quarters" if taught to read and write, "from the fourteenth day of September last past"

Hercules, James, "that Mauris Trent Brought In to this Country," servant to Thomas Withers, 3 October 1693, age 13, eight years servitude

Hood, Peter, servant to Henry Lewis, 14 September 1697, age 10, eleven years servitude

Houseek, Kenneth, servant to Peter Britton, 14 December 1697, age not adjudged, five years servitude "being he had been sick a while"

Hughin, John, servant to Samuel Milles (Meales), 14 December 1697, (age 15), "five years and a half" servitude, six years if taught to read and write, "from the 14th day of September last past"

Hunter, Saundy, male, servant to John Hanum, 9 June 1696, age not adjudged, five years servitude

Jack, Robert, servant to Philip Yarnell, 14 September 1697, age 13, eight years servitude

Johnson, James, "brought In by Maurice Trent," servant to Joseph Coeborn, 1 October 1695, age not adjudged, five years servitude

Johnstown, William, servant to Benjamin Mendinghall, 9 June 1696, (age 15), six years servitude

Leacy, George, "that Mauris Trent Brought In to this Country," servant to Nickoles Pile, 3 October 1693, age 12, nine years servitude

Levin, Andrew, servant to Thomas Hopes, 14 September 1697, (age 10), ten years servitude, eleven years if taught to read and write

COURT RECORDS, CHESTER COUNTY

Linn, George, servant to Thomas Reese, 14 September 1697, age 11,
 ten years servitude

Macdaniell, William, servant to Nicholes Newland, 5 October 1697, age 16,
 five years servitude, "five and a half" if taught to read and write,
 "from the 14th day of September last past"

Mack Deniell, Daniell, "that Mauris Trent Brought In to this Country,"
 servant to Richard Buffinton, 3 October 1693, age 14,
 seven years servitude

Mackellfray, John, "brought In by Maurice Trent," servant to Maurice Trent,
 1 October 1695, age not adjudged, five years servitude

Mackintoes, Daniell, servant to Hugh Williams, 5 October 1697, age 10,
 ten years servitude, eleven years if taught to read and write,
 "from the 14th day of September last"

Mac Klene, John, servant to David Harry, 14 September 1697, age 13,
 eight years servitude

Martin, John, servant to Goden (Godwin) Walter, 14 September 1697,
 age 11, ten years servitude

Mastertowne, James, servant to Randall Varnon, 14 September 1697,
 age 14, seven years servitude

Maston, John, servant to David Hugh, 14 December 1697, (age 13),
 eight years servitude "from the fourteenth day of September last"

Mecany, Alexander, "that Mauris Trent Brought In to this Country," servant
 to Jeremiah Collett, 3 October 1693, age 14, seven years servitude

Merscer, Robert, servant to Justice (John) Simcocke, 14 September 1697,
 age not adjudged, five years servitude

Mongey, Margaret, servant to Elizabeth Withers, 5 October 1697, age 11,
 ten years servitude, "from the 14th day of September last"

Moore, Allixander, servant to Robert Wade, 14 September 1697, age not
 adjudged, five years servitude

Nickles, Alexander, servant to John Howell, 14 September 1697, age 11,
 nine years servitude, ten years if taught to read and write

COURT RECORDS, CHESTER COUNTY

Nickols, Henery, "brought In by Maurice Trent," servant to John Kingsman, 1 October 1695, (age 13), eight years servitude

Norvill, Andrew, servant to John Cloud, 5 October 1697, age 15, six years servitude, "six years and a halfe" if taught to read or write, "from the fourteenth day of September last past"

Pruiss, George, servant to Lewis Walker, 14 September 1697, age 11, ten years servitude

Reese, Hugh, servant to Thomas Joans, 14 September 1697, age 11, ten years servitude

Robbinson, John, "brought in by Maurice Trent," servant to Thomas Cartwright, 10 December 1695, (age 13 1/2), "seven years and a halfe" servitude

Robbinson, John, servant to Nathaniel Richards, 5 October 1697, (age 10), ten years servitude, eleven years if taught to read and write, "from the 14th day of September last past"

Robbinson, Thomas, servant to Nathaniell Newland, 9 June 1696, (age 13), eight years servitude

Robertson, George, servant to Thomas Cartwright, 14 September 1697, age 16, five years servitude

Robison, John, servant to Justice (Jasper) Yeates, 14 September 1697, age not adjudged, five years servitude

Robinson, George, servant to John Bennitt, 9 June 1696, age not adjudged, five years servitude

Ross, Alexander, "that Mauris Trent Brought In to this Country,"servant to Caleb Pusye, 3 October 1693, age 11, ten years servitude

Royle, Mary, servant to Caleb Pusey, 14 September 1697, age not adjudged, five years servitude

Scott, Robart, servant to William Davis, 14 December 1697, age not adjudged, five years servitude "from the fourteenth day of September last past"

COURT RECORDS, CHESTER COUNTY

Simson, Magnis, "that Mauris Trent Brought In to this Country," servant to William Collett, 3 October 1693, age 11, ten years servitude

Sinkler, Robert, servant to John Crosby, 5 October 1697, (age 15), five years servitude, six years if taught to read and write, "from the 14th day of September last past"

Slaiter, John, servant to Evan Prother, 14 September 1697, (age 11), nine years servitude, to be taught to read

Sleder, John, servant to John Lewis Junior, 14 September 1697, age 12, nine years servitude

Steller, John, servant to Justice (John) Blunstone, 14 September 1697, (age 15), six years servitude

Steward, Alexander, servant to Francis Chadsey, 5 October 1697, (age 13), seven years servitude, eight years if taught to read or write, "from the 14th day of September last past"

Sunkly, William, servant to John Lewis Senior, 14 September 1697, age 11, ten years servitude

Taite, Magnis, male, servant to Evan Prother, 14 September 1697, (age 15), five years servitude, six years if taught to read

Taylor, Thomas, servant to Joseph Coeburn, 14 September 1697, age 11, ten years servitude

Thompson, Barbara, servant to Jeremiah Collett, 14 December 1697, age not adjudged, five years servitude

Trotter, Elizabeth, servant to Margaret Green, 14 December 1697, age not adjudged, five years servitude

Williamson, John, servant to Caleb Pusey, 14 September 1697, age 16, five years servitude

Woolson, Hugh, servant to John Morgan, 14 September 1697, age 12, nine years servitude

____, ____, female, servant to Morris Lewellin, 14 September 1697, age not adjudged, five years servitude

COURT RECORDS, CHESTER COUNTY

ASSIGNMENTS

Cormutt, Daniel, servant to James Hendrixson, assigned to William Brainton Junior, 12 March 1700

Driver, James, servant to William Collett "of Concord," assigned unto Thomas Worolaw "of Edgment," 12 December 1693

Robinson, George, servant to John Bennett, assigned to Richard Thatcher, 8 December 1696

Stewart, Alexander, former servant to Francis Chadsey, assigned to Henry Nayl, "and the said boy consents and agrees to serve the said Nayl one year and a quarter above his time by record if the said Henry Nayl teach hime the trade of a shoemaker," 10 June 1701

COURT RECORDS, BUCKS COUNTY

"Records of the Courts of Quarter Sessions and Common Pleas of Bucks County, Pennsylvania," 1684-1700
https://search.ancestry.com/search/db.aspx?dbid=14303

Barry, Robert, of Ireland, servant to James Plumley, 19 October 1699, age 10 "from this day," to serve "according to Law and at the expiration of his terme to have allowance accordingly."

Grant, Neel, servant to Joseph Kirkbride, 5 October 1697, age 13 "the first day of the fifth month Last past (1 May 1697), to serve "according to Law." "And the said Joseph Kirkbride promised to give to his Said Servant at the expiration of his terme as the Law directs."

Weire, John, servant to John Duncan, 5 October 1697, age 13 "from this day," to serve "according to Law." "And the said John Duncan promised to give to his Said Servant at the expiration of his terme of Servitude as the Law directs."

COURT RECORDS, BURLINGTON COUNTY

"The Burlington court book: a record of Quaker jurisprudence in West New Jersey," 1680-1709
https://search.ancestry.com/search/db.aspx?dbid=13867

Anderson, John, of Ireland, servant to James Shinn, "having newly bought him to serve until" the age of twenty-one, 20 February 1700, age 10, eleven years servitude.

Camrone, Daniell, of Scotland, servant to Abraham Heullings, who bought him on 21 July 1697 from James Trent, 9 August 1697, age not adjudged, nine years servitude, (age 12).

Douglass, George, of Scotland, servant to John Scott, who bought him on 21 July 1697 from James Trent, 9 August 1697, age not adjudged, nine years servitude, (age 12).

Gannington, Robert, servant to Hanna Wolston (Woolston) "Widdow," presented by William Cooper, 4 November 1700, "to be bound to her for Seven years from the time of his Arrival."

Haddgard, James, of Scotland, servant to Martin Scott, who bought him on 21 July 1697 from James Trent, 3 November 1697, age not adjudged, nine years servitude, (age 12).

MacCay, Daniel, of Ireland, servant to Restore Lippicut, "having newly bought him to serve until" the age of twenty-one, 20 February 1700, age 11, ten years servitude.

More, Benjamin, servant to Edward Ruckhill, who brought him from England, 21 December 1686, age 12 on "25th of the tenth Moneth 1686," to serve according to "the Custome of the Country."

Price, Rees, servant to Thomas Wallis, who bought him with Indentures dated 16 June 1698 from Richard Owen, 14 March 1699, to serve until age twenty-one in June 1704.

Slaiter, George, of Scotland, servant to John Lambert, who bought him on 21 July 1697 from James Trent, 9 August 1697, age not adjudged, nine years servitude, (age 12).

Young, John, of Scotland, servant to Thomas Lambert, who bought him on 21 July 1697 from James Trent, presented by Martin Scott, 3 November 1697, age not adjudged, nine years servitude, (age 12).

COURT RECORDS, KENT COUNTY

"Court Records of Kent County, Delaware, 1680-1705," edited by Leon DeValinger, Jr., State Archivist of Delaware, American Historical Association, Washington, D.C., 1959.

Adcock, Judith, 12 December 1699, age not stated, Samuell Barbary, ordered to serve "the terme of five years from the time of her arrivall which was the second day of May last past"

Cundon, Richard, 12 March 1700, age 12, John Walker, ordered to serve "untill he shall arrive to one and twenty years of age"

Gorden, Patrick, 13 June 1699, age 13, John Evans, ordered to serve "untill he shall arrive to one and twenty yeares of age"

Harbert, Thomas, 9 July 1700, age 17, Elizabeth Clifford, ordered to serve "untill he shall arrive to one and twenty yeares of age"

Linshey, Marcus, 13 June 1699, age 13, Thomas Bedwell, ordered to serve "untill he shall arrive to one and twenty yeares of age"

Linton, Nathaniell, 10 September 1700, age 17, William Nickolls, ordered to serve "five yeares commencinge from the two and twentyeth day of July last past"

Martin, James, 10 September 1700, age 17, William Nickolls, ordered to serve "five yeares commencinge from the two and twentyeth day of July last past"

Mattson, Aneus, 10 August 1697, age 14, Robert Hudson, sentence not stated

Raymour, Thomas, 12 September 1699, age 14, Robert Bedwell, ordered to serve "untill he shall arrive to one and twenty years of age"

Red, John, 9 November 1697, age 18, Richard Willson, ordered to serve five years "commencinge from the midle of July last, about which time he arrived in this Country"

Scott, Georg, 14 September 1698, age 15 "and foure months," Samuel Berry, ordered "to serve till he be one and twenty years of age"

Simpson, William, 12 December 1699, age 13 "and six months," John Walker, ordered to serve "untill he shall arrive to one and twenty years of age"

BAPTISMAL RECORDS

Bullen, Thomas, son of Nathaniel Bullen, Baptized 13 October 1682,
 St. Peter, Chester, Cheshire, England
Bullen, Thomas, servant to Henery Worlye, 9 June 1696, (age 14),
 seven years servitude. Chester County

Clunie, William, son of James Clunie.,Baptized 2 January 1687,
 Errol, Perth, Scotland
Clowney, William, servant to John Redmeall, 5 October 1697, age 10,
 ten years servitude, eleven years if taught to read and write,
 "from the 14th day of September last" Chester County

Dobie, Lydias, son of James Dobie and Elizabeth Reid, Baptized
 10 August 1680, Edinburgh Parish, Edinburgh, Scotland
Dobie, Lydias, male, servant to Jasper Yeates, 10 March 1696, (age 15),
 six years servitude. Chester County

Finley, Margaret, daughter of Robert Finley, Baptized 4 May 1684,
 All Saints, Newcastle upon Tyne, Northumberland, England
Finley, Margaret, servant to John Sharpley, 14 September 1697,
 age 13, eight years servitude. Chester County

Flett, Robert, son of Thomas Flett and Isabel Frazer, Baptized
 24 January 1681, Kirkwall, Orkney, Scotland
Flatt, Robert, "brought In by Maurice Trent," servant to Maurice Trent,
 1 October 1695, (age 13), eight years servitude. Chester County

Fraser, Androw, son of Donald Fraser, Baptized 4 February 1677,
 Inverness, Inverness, Scotland
Fraisor, Andrew, "brought In by Maurice Trent," servant to Francis Baldwin,
 1 October 1695, age not adjudged, five years servitude
 [would have been at least sixteen years of age] Chester County

Frizall, Alexander, son of William Frizall, Baptized 26 September 1684,
 Ratho (near Edinburgh), Midlothian, Scotland
Freezell, Alexander, servant to William Thomas, 14 December 1697,
 (age 14), "six years and a half" servitude, seven years if taught
 to read and write, "from the fourteenth day of September last"
 Chester County

BAPTISMAL RECORDS

Johnstowne, William, son of James Johnstowne, Baptized 16 October 1683,
  Colinton, Edinburgh, Scotland
Johnstown, William, servant to Benjamin Mendinghall, 9 June 1696,
  (age 15), six years servitude. Chester County

Lacy, George, son of Roger Lacy, Baptized 19 December 1682,
  Okehampton, Devon, England
Leacy, George, "that Mauris Trent Brought In to this Country," servant to
  Nickoles Pile, 3 October 1693, age 12, nine years servitude
  Chester County

Maston, John, son of James and Susan Maston, Baptized 20 May 1685,
  Saint Dunstan in the East, London, England
Maston, John, servant to David Hugh, 14 December 1697, (age 13),
  eight years servitude "from the fourteenth day of September last"
  Chester County

Nicholls, Henry, son of Richard and Margaret Nicholls, Baptized
  22 March 1681, Coldridge, Devon, England
Nickols, Henery, "brought In by Maurice Trent," servant to John Kingsman,
  1 October 1695, (age 13), eight years servitude. Chester County

Seller, John, son of Alexander Seller and Margaret Penman, Baptized
  22 December 1682, Airth, Stirling, Scotland
Steller, John, servant to Justice (John) Blunstone, 14 September 1697,
  (age 15), six years servitude. Chester County

Symondsone, Magnus, son of Edward Symondsone and Elspet Craigie,
  Baptized 14 October 1680, Kirkwall, Orkney, Scotland
Simson, Magnis, "that Mauris Trent Brought In to this Country," servant to
  William Collett, 3 October 1693, age 11, ten years servitude
  Chester County

Tait, Magnus, Baptized 1681 or 1682, Kirkwall, Orkney, Scotland
  [several by this name in this parish, nowhere else in all of Scotland]
Taite, Magnis, male, servant to Evan Prother, 14 September 1697, (age 15),
  five years servitude, six years if taught to read. Chester County

Willson, Hugh, son of Lewis and Jane Willson, Baptized 15 June 1684,
  Saint Peter Cornhill, London, England
Woolson, Hugh, servant to John Morgan, 14 September 1697, age 12,
  nine years servitude. Chester County

BAPTISMAL RECORDS

John, son of John Anderson, gent, & Elizabeth, his wife, Baptized
 Oct. ye 21st, 1691, Church of Saint Michan's, Dublin, Ireland
Anderson, John, of Ireland, servant to James Shinn, "having newly bought
 him to serve until" the age of twenty-one, 20 February 1700, age 10,
 eleven years servitude. Burlington County

More, Benjamin, son of John and Repentance More, Baptized
 28 February 1672, Saint James, Clerknenwell, London, England
More, Benjamin, servant to Edward Ruckhill, who brought him from
 England, 21 December 1686, age 12 on "25th of the tenth Moneth
 1686," to serve according to "the Custome of the Country."
 Burlington County

Price, Reese, son of William and Judeth Price, Baptized 1 April 1680,
 Saint Paul Covent Garden, Westminster, London, England
Price, Rees, servant to Thomas Wallis, who bought him with Indentures
 dated 16 June 1698 from Richard Owen, 14 March 1699, to serve
 until age twenty-one in June 1704. Burlington County

NOTES ON OTHER SURNAMES

Mattson, Aneus, 10 August 1697, age 14, Robert Hudson, sentence not stated

[brought to Kent County, Delaware; ref. *"Birth and Shipping Records,"* p. 372]

The western coast of Scotland and the desolate Hebrides islands are the ancient home of the Mattson family.

Hercules, James, "that Mauris Trent Brought In to this Country," servant to
 Thomas Withers, 3 October 1693, age 13, eight years servitude

[brought to Chester County, Pennsylvania]

The surname of Hercules is found in Scotland and Shetland, mainly in the parishes of Lunnasting and Tingwell.

Camrone, Daniell, of Scotland, servant to Abraham Heullings, who bought
 him on 21 July 1697 from James Trent, 9 August 1697, age not
 adjudged, nine years servitude, (age 12).

[brought to Burlington County, New Jersey]

The rugged west coast of Scotland and the desolate Hebrides islands are the ancestral home of the Cameron family.

MARRIAGE RECORDS

Allen, Elizabeth, servant to John Wood, 5 October 1697, age not adjudged, five years servitude. Chester County
Elizabeth Allen, married Samuel Addams, 16 May 1704, St. Paul's Episcopal Church, Chester, Delaware, Pennsylvania

Conner, Margaret, servant to Justice (Jasper) Yeates, 14 September 1697, age not adjudged, five years servitude. Chester County
Margaret Conner, married Andrew Johnson, 14 December 1712, Christ Church, Philadelphia, Pennsylvania

Freezell, Alexander, servant to William Thomas, 14 December 1697, (age 14), "six years and a half" servitude, seven years if taught to read and write, "from the fourteenth day of September last" Chester County
Alexander Frazell, married Rebecca Walton, 10 January 1704, Marblehead, Essex, Massachusetts

More, Benjamin, servant to Edward Ruckhill, who brought him from England, 21 December 1686, age 12 on "25th of the tenth Moneth 1686," to serve according to "the Custome of the Country." Burlington County
Benjamin More, married Sarah Stoakes, intentions 4 November 1693, Burlington Monthly Meeting, Burlington County, New Jersey

Nickols, Henery, "brought In by Maurice Trent," servant to John Kingsman, 1 October 1695, (age 13), eight years servitude. Chester County
Henry Nichols, married Elizabeth Gatchell, 17 April 1707, St. Paul's Episcopal Church, Chester, Delaware, Pennsylvania

Price, Rees, servant to Thomas Wallis, who bought him with Indentures dated 16 June 1698 from Richard Owen, 14 March 1699, to serve until age twenty-one in June 1704. Burlington County
Rice Price, married Sarah More, intentions 3 November 1705, Radnor Monthly Meeting, Delaware, Pennsylvania
Rece Price, married Elizabeth Elis, intentions 9 November 1718, Radnor Monthly Meeting, Delaware, Pennsylvania

Robertson, George, servant to Thomas Cartwright, 14 September 1697, age 16, five years servitude. Chester County
George Robertson, married Widow Sarah Hall, May 10, 1708, St. Paul's Episcopal Church, Chester, Delaware, Pennsylvania

MARRIAGE RECORDS

Ross, Alexander, "that Mauris Trent Brought In to this Country,"servant to Caleb Pusye, 3 October 1693, age 11, ten years servitude. Chester County
Elixander Ross,, married Katherin Chambers, intentions 25 March 1706, Chester Monthly Meeting, Providence, Chester, Pennsylvania

Royle, Mary, servant to Caleb Pusey, 14 September 1697, age not adjudged, five years servitude. Chester County
Married (1): William Cole of Nottingham; (2) Jeremiah Brown, intentions 12 March 1711, Concord Monthly Meeting, Chester, Pennsylvania

Sinkler, Robert, servant to John Crosby, 5 October 1697, (age 15), five years servitude, six years if taught to read and write, "from the 14th day of September last past" Chester County
Robert Sinclair, married Mary Coppock, daughter of Aaron Coppock, intentions 15 February 1712, New Garden Monthly Meeting, Chester County, Pennsylvania

Steward, Alexander, servant to Francis Chadsey, 5 October 1697, (age 13), seven years servitude, eight years if taught to read or write, "from the 14th day of September last past" Chester County
Alexander Stewart, married Mary Baily, daughter of Joel Baily and Ann Short, c. 1706, Pennsylvania
Jane Stuart, daughter of Alex and Mary Stewart, Born August 1709, Chester, Delaware, Pennsylvania
Robert Stuart, daughter of Alexander and Mary Stuart, Born 25 January 1710, Kennett Township, Chester County, Pennsylvania
Alexander Stewart, Will Dated 30 October 1714, Will Proved 20 April 1715

["Mary, daughter of Joel and Ann Baily and widow of Alexander Stewart of Kennett,", married George Harlan, 1715]

Taite, Magnis, male, servant to Evan Prother, 14 September 1697, (age 15), five years servitude, six years if taught to read, Chester County
Magnes Tate, married Honor Williams, 29 March 1714, St. Paul's Episcopal Church, Chester, Delaware, Pennsylvania

Thompson, Barbara, servant to Jeremiah Collett, 14 December 1697, age not adjudged, five years servitude. Chester County
Barbara Thompson, married George Grant, 19 July 1702, First Presbyterian Church, Philadelphia, Pennsylvania

SURNAME INDEX

Abrams	67	Bell	14, 45	Bull	37
Adams, Addams		Bellamy	14, 35	Bullen	69, 78
	1, 6, 20, 81	Bendall	4	Bulling	42
Adcock	6, 77	Benjamin	67	Bullott	10
Ailer, Eyler	6	Bennett	73, 75	Burkett	30
Albritton	33	Benson	16	Burleigh	41
Alexander	10, 42, 52	Bent	37	Burnham	17
Allen	69, 81	Berks, Burke	7, 8	Butler	33
Allie	41	Big, Bigs	26	Cage	25
Amis	26	Bigelow	67	Cameron	76, 80
Anderson	6, 13,	Bing	9, 10	Cammell	8, 46
	19, 76, 80	Bisse, Bissey	33	Campion	23
Andrus	49	Black	51	Canady	38, 69
Arnall, Arnold		Blandon	41	Cane, Canes	8
	1, 6, 52, 68	Bloustowne	69	Cant	37, 52
Ashton	26	Blunstone	74, 79	Carding	43
Atchison	52	Blunt	6	Carlton	7
Atkins	20, 41	Booth	26	Carpenter	23
Atkinson	50	Bosse	49	Carr	10, 12
Attwood	1	Bourne	27	Carter	12, 15, 18,
Atty	37	Bowler	41		19, 20, 24, 32, 52, 69
Austin	2, 7	Bowling	31	Cartwright	73, 81
Backler, Backter	52	Bowman	52, 68	Causine	17, 31, 44
Badell	16	Bradley	52	Chacrett, Sacrett	48
Baily, Bayley	43, 82	Bradshaw	14, 49	Chadsey	69, 74, 75, 82
Baker	1, 7, 11, 26, 49	Braine	41	Chambers	20, 27, 69, 82
Baldwin	69, 70, 78	Brainton	75	Chandler	44
Ball	50	Breezer	69	Chapman	52
Ballister	7	Brereton	27	Cherman	30
Barbary	77	Bridge, Bridges	27	Chester	42
Barrick	7	Bridgeman	7, 68	Chilton	15, 34
Barry, Berry		Bright	27	Chisman	9
	75, 77	Britton	71	Churchill	42
Barton	7, 24	Broadhead	52	Clark	1
Barwick	48	Brooke, Brookes		Clary	42
Batcheller	33		8, 23, 67	Claypoole	68
Batt	50	Brown, Browne		Clements	9, 52
Baxter	24, 26		20, 52, 71, 82	Clems, Clews	52
Bayne	16	Bruce	69	Clifford	77
Beackly	69	Brumskill	52	Cloud	73
Beale, Beall	15, 47, 52	Bryan	23, 38	Clunie	70, 78
Bean, Beane	15, 69	Bryant	37	Coats	3
Beckingham	37	Buckle	50	Cobreath	8
Bedwell	77	Buffinton	72		

SURNAME INDEX

Coeborn, Coeburn	71, 74	Davis	20, 22, 42, 67, 69, 73	Elzey	53
Coffey, Covey	8	Dawson	27, 42	English	21, 28
Colclough	18, 34	Day	67	Estington	2
Cole, Collie	9, 42, 82	Deakins	51	Evans	10, 77
Collett	69, 70, 72, 74, 75, 79, 82	Dell	53	Evelling, Evoling	9, 53
		Dennett	10, 18	Everatt	28
Collier	50	Denny	27, 35	Eyres	27
Collonon	32	Dent	29, 39	Falconer	51
Combes	46	Derby	35	Faucett	53
Consett	52	Dermott	53	Fendall	31
Conner	70, 81	Devenish	37	Ferrendyne	50
Conway	52	Dickinson	18	Fewell	9
Cook, Cooke	68	Dill	37	Fielding	46
Cooper	33, 53, 68, 76	Ditton	70	Fifield	3
Cope	71	Dixon	34, 44	Finch	21
Coppock	82	Dobbins	20	Finley	70, 78
Cormutt	70, 75	Dobie	70, 78	Finney	36
Corbet	27	Doell	70	Fisher	4, 28
Corbin, Corbyn	19, 41	Dollen, Dollins	42	Flatt, Flett	70, 78
Cotteroll	38	Doman, Dowman	28	Flax	51
Coursey	7	Douglass	76	Fletcher	53, 67
Court	27	Dowell	9, 23	Flint	67
Cousins	33	Draper	9	Foote	10
Coutanceau	44	Drew, Drewe	33, 53	Ford	38, 43
Covell	53	Driver	70, 75	Foster	33
Cox	41	Dudley	11, 53	Fowke	8
Craigie	79	Duffee, Tuffe	9	Fowler	1, 10
Crane	9	Dugles	70	Fox	49, 67
Crawley	34	Duncan	75	Foxcroft	23
Creech	49	Dunderdell	27	Fraisor, Fraser, Frazer	70, 78
Creeke	53	Dunford	38	Frank	43
Cressop	50	Dutch	49	Franklin	7
Crew	3	Dyal	9	Frazell, Freezell, Frizell	28, 70, 78, 81
Crookshanks	53	Dymond	68		
Crosby	74, 82	Earle	13	Freeman	10, 29
Cundey, Cundie	42	Eason	42	Fuller	67
Cundon	77	Easter	28	Furly	3
Cunningham	70	Eborne	46	Furnifull	48
Daton, Deaton	27	Edgate, Edgett	53	Gabb	3
David, Davids	27	Edwards	25, 53	Gannington	76
Davidson	70	Elgin	9	Garlington	8
Davies	20	Ellis	21, 53, 81	Gary	13
		Ells	53	Gatchell	81

SURNAME INDEX

Gaton	10	Hagar, Hager	67	Hone	2
Geery	48	Hall	54, 81	Hood	71
Gibb, Gibbs	34, 70	Hambleton	47, 49	Hopes	71
Gibbons	1	Hamlyn	48	Hopkins	11, 54
Gilbert	23, 28, 38	Hancock	21, 23	Hopper	68
Giles	34	Hankes, Hincks	11	Hornold	48
Gill	43, 48	Hanson	31	Hosier	46
Gilson	21	Hanum	71	Houseek	71
Ginge, Ginges	53	Harbert	77	Howell	72
Glascock	43	Harbey	11	Hownsden	49
Goar	53	Harper	71	Hudson	67, 68, 77, 80
Goble	28	Harris	23, 54	Hugh	72, 79
Godby	38	Harry, Herry	11, 72	Hughes	2
Goldsmith	18	Hartley	51	Hughin	71
Gooch	37	Hartwell	67	Hunt	5
Goodge	31	Haskins	22	Hunter	71
Goodrick	44	Hasted	54	Hurd	29
Gorden, Gordon		Hatch	28	Hutchins	21
	29, 71, 77	Hatton	11	Irons	40
Gore	50	Haverland	49	Ismett	1
Gosh	10	Hawkins	30	Jack	71
Gough	13	Hayes	2, 24, 68	Jackson	22, 39, 51, 54
Grady	43	Hazard	38	Jacob, Jacobs	34
Grant	28, 75, 82	Hazelwood	54	James	24, 35, 54
Grantham	18, 25, 53	Heald	67	Janson	54
Graves	47	Heathcott	33	Jarman	70
Gray	38, 49	Hendrickson	70, 75	Jefferies, Jeffreys	
Green, Greene		Hensley	49		2, 10, 35, 54, 68
	2, 53, 74	Hercules	71, 80	Jenifer	15
Greenwater	71	Heullings	76, 80	Jenkins	3, 12
Greenway	2, 34, 68	Hewes, Hughes	11	Joans	71, 73
Greeve	71	Hewett	16	Jobson	12
Gregory	10, 49	Hewlett	50	Johnson	12, 15,
Griffin	43	Hewson, Huson	12		29, 54, 71, 81
Griggs	29	Heynes	21	Johnstown	71, 79
Grimes	34	Hicks	21	Jones	3, 17, 19, 24, 54
Groome	38	Hide	12, 54	Jordan	12
Grove, Groves	10, 54	Hilson	54	Joyce	43
Gunn	50	Hinsey	33	Jury	30, 54
Gutteridge	54	Hitchcock	34	Keane, Keene	13, 44
Guy	29, 34	Hobbs	54	Keelby, Kilbee	12
Gwyn	51	Holloway	24	Kelly	24
Hackett	38	Holly	3	Kelsick	54
Haddgard	76	Homan	43	Kemp, Kempe	13, 14

SURNAME INDEX

Kennedy	46	Ludow	21	Morgan	
Kenney, Kenny	13	MacCay	76		3, 14, 55, 74, 79
Kent	24, 29, 50	Macey	43	Morland	39
King	24, 29, 30, 43	Mackeel	13	Morrell	44
Kingsman	73, 79, 81	Mackellfray	72	Morris	50
Kirkbride	75	Mac Klene	72	Mortimer	44
Kirton	14	Mackrorey	32	Morton	14, 30
Knight	3, 38	Maddox	8, 35	Moseley	14, 55
Lacy, Leacy	71, 79	Male, Maley	13	Mugg	14
Lamb	51	Malson	1	Munro	35
Lambert	23, 29, 50, 76	Mann	46, 55	Murphy	46
Lampton	31	Manning	35, 46	Musgrove	30
Lane	3	Mar, Mare	13	Mustin, Muston	35
Larimore	55	Marshall	28, 55	Navarr	25
Lashbrooke	55	Martin, Martyn	11, 14,	Nayl	75
Lattinoe	50		25, 38, 39, 55, 72	Neale	3, 4, 23, 36, 47
Lawrence	13, 38, 39	Mason	3, 21, 30	Nell	15
Lawson	46	Mastertowne	72	Nevill	45
Laycock	55	Maston	72, 79	Newell	14
Leach	55, 67	Mattson	77, 80	Newland	72, 73
Lee	17, 48	Mathews	24	Newman	12, 21, 24, 30
Lennell	23	Mayline	49	Newton	1, 44
Levin	71	McCoy	55	Nichols, Nickels	14, 30
Lewellin	74	McDaniel	46, 72		42, 72, 73, 77, 79, 81
Lewgar	24	McIntosh	72	Noble	18
Lewis	71, 74	Meade	50	Nock	8, 14
Librey	26	Mecany	72	Nonna, Nun	31
Lily, Lilly	30	Medford	55	Norris	44
Lindow	6, 55	Medley	48	Norvill	73
Lines, Lynes	9, 38	Meer, Mere	13	Nutt	7
Linn	72	Mendinghall	71, 79	Nutter	21
Linshey	77	Mercer	72	Omaly	31, 36
Linton	77	Meredith	37, 69	Orpitt, Allpitt	48
Lippicut	76	Merriman	27	Orton	55
Little	35	Middleton	51	Osborn, Osburne	15
Lloyd, Loyd	24	Miles	3, 71	Ould, Old	15
Loch	55	Millett	67	Overton	49
Long	25	Mills	25, 71	Owen	42, 76, 81
Lovell	8	Minchon	21	Pagan	55
Lowe, Lows	24, 55	Mongey	72	Page	15
Lowens	70	Monke	30	Paine	15
Lucam, Lucan	55	Montfort	14	Painter	4
Lucas	8	Moore. More		Palmer	21
Luckett	15, 16		55, 68, 72, 76, 80, 81	Parke	35

SURNAME INDEX

Parker	9, 25, 49	Price	4, 22, 34,	Rye	16
Parly	4		50, 51, 76, 80, 81	St. Leger Codd	11
Parramore	39	Prinn, Prynne	56	Salisbury	16
Parrott	18, 35	Prother	74, 79, 82	Sander, Sanders	16
Parson, Parsons		Prouce	26	Sands	49
	10, 21, 55	Pruiss	73	Sanster	33
Partridge	51	Pruitt	36	Sargeant	56
Pawsson	29	Purvis	56	Saunders	34
Payne	68	Pusey	73, 74, 82	Scarborough	27, 37
Peacock	55	Ransom, Ranson	45, 56	Schreever	34
Pearce, Peirce	22, 55, 56	Raymour	77	Scott	40, 73, 76, 77
Pearle	31	Read, Reade, Reed, Reid		Seabrell	13, 16
Pearson	25		4, 28, 68, 78	Sech	21
Penman	79	Reading, Redinge	4, 16	Self	34
Penn	15, 68	Red	77	Seller, Steller	74, 79
Pennell	70	Redford	32	Servant	51
Pensax	56	Redman	16	Shaile	4
Perk, Perke	12, 16	Redmeall	70, 78	Shakespeare	1
Perkins	4, 15, 25	Reene, Renes	31	Sharp, Sharpe	25, 41, 48
Perks, Pirks	44	Reese	72, 73	Sharpley	70, 78
Peters	35	Reilly, Riley	36	Shaw	25, 31
Peterson	9	Revell	42	Sheers	19
Phage	49	Rhodes	56	Sheppard	33
Phelps	4	Richards	73	Shinn	76, 80
Phillips	69	Richardson	11	Shipp	6
Picket	28	Rider	33, 56	Simcocke	72
Picks	56	Riddiford	4	Simmons	16
Piggen	3	Riddle	39, 49	Simons	50
Pile	71, 79	Roberts	22, 25	Simpson	17, 31, 77
Pinchbeck	45	Robertson	73, 81	Sims	39
Piper	35	Robinson	41, 73, 75	Simson	74, 79
Pitt	43	Robison	73	Sinclair, Sinkler	74, 82
Player	36	Rock	56	Sinners	56
Plover	56	Rogers	9, 44, 49	Skinner	68
Plumley	75	Rose, Rosier	44	Slaiter, Sleder	
Plunkett	46	Ross	73, 82		74, 76
Poke, Pook	39	Rowland	25	Slingsby	49, 50
Poor, Poore	16, 29	Royle	73, 82	Smallwood	27, 44
Potts	31	Rozer	40	Smith, Smyth	
Poulter	36	Ruckhill	76, 80, 81		4, 17, 20, 56
Pratt	16, 49	Rudd	50	Spann	46
Preeson	68	Russell, Russells	16, 50	Speding	56
Presly	26	Rust	31	Spenser	5
Preston	46, 49	Rutter	39	Spry	56

SURNAME INDEX

Surname	Pages
Stanley	17
Staples	49
Steedman	17
Stephens, Stevens	1, 13, 18, 68
Sterne	19
Steward, Stewart, Stuart	74, 75, 82
Still, Stille	32
Stoakes	81
Stone	49
Stott	8
Stringer	56
Sturey	5
Styles	17
Sumner	49
Sunkly	74
Sutton	56
Swann, Swanne	10, 18
Symonds	57
Tait, Taite	74, 79, 82
Taylor	17, 33, 57, 74
Tedder	50
Tenth	57
Thatcher	75
Therriatt	6, 29
Thew, Thewe	49, 50
Thilman	37
Thomas	17, 57, 70, 78, 81
Thompson	74, 82
Thornton	47, 57
Thorp	68
Thwait	11
Tibbetts	39, 57
Tony	44
Towers	51
Townsend	9, 12
Toy, Toye	44
Tracey	5
Travers	35
Trent	69, 70, 71, 72, 73, 74, 76, 78, 79, 81, 82
Trigany	6, 57
Trim, Trimm	51, 57
Trott	31
Trotter	74
Tubb	39
Tullos	36
Tyson	32
Upton	5, 47
Vanfleeten	57
Varbell	57
Varnon	72
Vaughan	18
Vaus	7
Videll	57
Wade	7, 39, 43, 72
Waddy	7
Wakefield	32
Wale, Wayle	32
Walker	20, 46, 73, 77
Walkup	67
Wallis	76, 80, 81
Walter	45, 72
Walton	81
Ward	45
Warner	45, 57
Warren	42, 57
Warwicke	24
Wasey	68
Washbourne	36
Waters	25, 30, 36
Watson	18
Watts	18, 25, 43
Webb	1, 18, 20
Webber	57
Weedon	43
Weire	75
Welton, Wilton	22
Wheeler	11, 67
Wheelock	57
Wheldon, Whilden	18
Whiffin, Wiffin	18
White	5, 18, 39
Whiteside	57
Whit, Whitt	40
Whittington	28
Whysken	16
Wickes	12
Wigginton	36
Wilcox	33
Wild, Wyld	18, 41
Wildey	35
Wilkings	57
Williams	19, 20, 72, 82
Williamson	74
Willis	57
Willmot	19, 49
Wilson, Woolson	19, 74, 77, 79
Wine, Wyne	6
Wintersell	17
Wise	57
Withers	71, 72, 80
Wolston, Woolston	76
Wood	19, 49, 69, 81
Woodman	19, 40
Woodmansee	69
Woolles	5
Worolaw	75
Worlye	69, 78
Wormeley	32
Worrell	70
Wortham	39
Yarnell	71
Yeates	70, 73, 78, 81
Yoe	57
Young	48, 57, 76

www.ingramcontent.com/pod-product-compliance
Lightning Source LLC
Chambersburg PA
CBHW070949180426
43194CB00041B/1958